BREAKING THE
BLOCKBUSTER
MODEL

USING EDTECH AND ACCESSIBILITY TO "SEE WHAT'S NEXT" IN CLASSROOMS

NATE RIDGWAY

Special discounts are available on quantity purchases by schools, school districts, associations, and others. Email books@daveburgessconsulting.com for pricing and details.

Published by Ditch That Textbook, whose printing operation is a division of Dave Burgess Consulting, Inc.

DitchThatTextbook.com
DaveBurgessConsulting.com
Cover design and interior design by Najdan Mancic, Iskon Design Inc.
Proofreading by Mairead Beeson
Developmental editing by Matt Miller
Icons used with permission via The Noun Project

Library of Congress Control Number: 2022938173

Paperback ISBN: 978-1-956306-27-9
Ebook ISBN: 978-1-956306-25-5
First printing: May 2022

To B.L.R, and L.R.R, and to all of those who will teach them.

TABLE OF CON

COPPA AND FERPA NOTICE

Before trying new apps or devices in your classroom, make sure you have studied both COPPA (Children's Online Privacy Protection Act) and FERPA (Family Educational Rights and Privacy Act) guidelines for use with K–12 students and their alignment with your particular school's policies. The US Department of Education provides suggestions at: studentprivacy.ed.gov.

PREQUEL

"Is this a 2-Day or a 7-Day Rental?"
—Every Blockbuster Checkout, Ever.

As a millennial, I can distinctly remember the feeling of walking into a Blockbuster. Remember those endless rows of DVDs and VHS? And that you could rent video game consoles? How about that feeling when you got home and your rental had the wrong movie inside the case? Or the dread when the young teenage employee behind the counter said that you had an outstanding late fee?

Blockbuster is a weird thing to feel nostalgia for, especially in our current age of Netflix, Amazon Prime, YouTube, and Twitch. But, for its time, it was, in a word, transformative. It felt like Blockbuster opened a new world. Never before could we find such a vast range of movies so close to home— just around the corner—and bring those titles home to our living room.

Now, as a social studies teacher, I reflect on how transformative that moment was and immediately think of a
similarly transformative historical parallel: the Market
Revolutions, which happened in the mid-19th century.
Rivers, once thought of as only unidirectional, became
two-directional steamboat highways. Canals and railroad
lines cut into the continent's topography, leaving scars in
the landscape, only to be bandaged over decades later by
ribbons of asphalt for automobiles.

But there was one invention during this time that
stands out: the American telegraph, the first machine
capable of sending a message over a single wire. In 1844,
its inventor, Samuel. B. Morse tested his new invention by
sending this message: "WHAT HATH GOD WROUGHT?"
His query, a reference to Numbers 23:23 in the Bible, was
a prophetic choice. He and his contemporaries faced a
proverbial (pun intended) flood of innovation and change.
What followed was the challenge to make sense of it and
harness it for good.

First Telegraphic Message—24 May 1844. Samuel Finley Breese Morse Papers at
the Library of Congress, 1793 to 1919. Manuscript Division

This book is a modern-day, edu-themed meditation
on Morse's question. Classrooms since the year 2000
have witnessed a deluge of change, everything from *No
Child Left Behind* to COVID-19. So, in light of all of the
changes we've experienced in teaching and learning, **the**

question is: how can we *understand where we've been to* further *understand where we should go next?*

This is where the Blockbuster metaphor comes in. While it changed the way we consumed and interacted with media in the 90s and 2000s (like the telegraph did in the 1800s), only a single Blockbuster store is left as of 2022. Something's changed. *Breaking the Blockbuster Model* explores if our classrooms should change, too. And if so, how?

My motivation for writing this book is the water in which I swim: teaching. COVID-19 and the persistence of systemic educational inequities in the US fueled a fire in me—and educators around the nation. A serious examination of long-standing approaches to teaching and learning is sorely needed. As teachers and students re-entered our classrooms post-pandemic, many have looked for a "return to normal." Instead, I think it's time to ask if normal is worth returning to.

Let's quickly get one thing straight: this book isn't a "silver bullet" solution to every problem we currently, or ever will, face as educators. I would love, for instance, for this book to fix long-standing pay inequity, our long hours, or the serious shortage of coffee in our lives. But as an eighth-year teacher with depression and anxiety, I firmly believe that any professional help I can offer a fellow educator is a victory for our mental health. Let's leave the silver bullet solutions for werewolf flicks.

At the same time, though, rethinking how our classrooms should work won't be easy or comfortable. For me, it means challenging assumptions I held as a first-year teacher, and even as far back as being a K–12 student myself. **Transformation can—and, arguably, should—take some thought and time.** Improvement works better when it comes from **evolution**, not **revolution**. Evolution is purposeful and methodical; revolution is aimless and stressful. That's why this book isn't intended to serve as another "dish" to add to educators' plates. That approach doesn't work—just ask any teacher who's been bombarded by "Flavor-of-the-Month" professional development where they're bounced from trend to trend.

This book also isn't going to be just a bunch of theories or just a bunch of strategies: it's both! One of the main problems I've encountered as a teacher is that **we rarely get solid research paired with practical strategies or vice-versa.** We either get the theory with no concrete examples to implement or modify for our own use, or we're inundated with tools and activities that have no research to back them up. In either scenario, we're left feeling like a movie with no plot, unsure what's working or where we're going. **My goal is to empower your teaching by pairing research with practicality** so when you're designing that next lesson or having a conversation with a parent about your LMS (learning management system), you know what you're doing is best for you and your students—especially in terms of learning outcomes, equity, and access.

In short, good change comes from sustained introspection and empowering teachers with the research and tools to make a positive difference. This book aims to do just that.

Every teacher brings their own philosophical perspectives to the classroom. This book is no different. I owe much of my worldview to the efforts of extremely talented individuals and organizations that deserve credit beyond what words can capture. In the interests of full disclosure, these persons and models influence my teaching practices—and this book—heavily:

- Carol Ann Tomlinson's work on differentiation.

- CAST's Universal Design for Learning (UDL) model, which focuses extensively on issues of access.

- Pooja Agarwal and Patrice Bain's book, *Powerful Teaching*, on retrieval practices and meaningful learning.

- My first book, *Don't Ditch That Tech*, by Dr. Angelia Ridgway (my mom!), Matt Miller, and myself.

You'll find the following pages full of activities and lessons I use as a high school social studies teacher. If you teach other subjects, ages (elementary, middle school, or collegiate students), or through other apps, don't worry! Lots of these ideas can be adapted for your particular needs. Plus, many dedicated educators from a wide variety of backgrounds have graced the following pages with examples from their own classrooms.

Before going on, let's establish a few underlying "absolutes" about one reoccurring topic, educational technology (edtech), before getting to our first chapter, "The Movie Theater Model." These principles are taken directly from *Don't Ditch That Tech* (Miller, Ridgway, and Ridgway 2019), a book I co-authored:

1. Technology should be used to enhance students' learning and should rely on evidence-based practices. There is simply no substitute for great teaching or great student–teacher relationships.

2. Technology should help us work with content in interactive, meaningful ways.

3. Technology should help teachers and students cross varied developmental levels.

4. Technology should eventually empower students to be designers of their own learning. The goal is for students to become critical thinkers and life-long learners.

5. Technology should promote reflection and metacognition.

Just as in *Don't Ditch That Tech* (2019), you'll see that edtech forms an integral part of this book, too. With that in mind, let's also acknowledge what edtech cannot or should not do. Edtech cannot be:

1. Done for the sake of itself. Tech is **not** the learning goal. Just because an app or cool feature exists doesn't mean it should be used.

2. Implemented without support and structure. Every successful educator and student needs a host of wrap-around services to make their work possible.

3. Executed without planning and preparation. Good teaching comes from good practice and subsequent reflection (a combination known as *praxis).*

With this foundational footing in mind, let's get a glimpse of what's coming up next:

- **CHAPTER 1: The Movie Theater Model** introduces you to the first third of this book's central metaphor: the movie theater. Through this lens, we'll explore how a teacher-centered classroom shows up in our everyday teaching and analyze its strengths and weaknesses. As you'll see, this model isn't necessarily wrong or ineffective, but it is in need of some major renovations and should be used sporadically.

- **CHAPTER 2: The Sequel: Getting the Most out of Movie Theater Moments** dives into countless strategies, examples, and how-to's from amazingly talented educators who utilize those brief nickelodeon moments to the maximum.

- **CHAPTER 3: The Blockbuster Model** continues the metaphor, featuring, of course, Blockbuster! Blockbuster represents many of the things considered "traditional" in the classroom outside of a teacher-centered curriculum, from textbooks to approaches to late work. We'll look at what recent research tells us and consult some experts.

■ **CHAPTER 4: Spinoff Series: Getting the Most from Blockbuster Moments** gets into more tangible and practical explorations of the Blockbuster Model with tips and tricks for your own classroom.

■ **CHAPTER 5: The Streaming Model** is the last chapter of the book and introduces us to the evolution of pedagogy towards a more student-centric, accessible, and equitable system for teaching and learning. It also shows off the efforts of real educators to create these opportunities for students.

Watch out for "plot points" and "plot twists." The plot points show today's reality, highlighting some of the concerns with the status quo. The plot twists offer some solutions and glimpses at possible new realities.

Then, as we paint a picture of what the future could be in Chapter 5, you'll find the plot points and the twists together. That way, you'll get a concrete path forward, a solution right after reading about the current reality.

And with that ... lights, camera, action!

—Nate

CHAPTER ONE

The Movie Theater Model

Movie theater: "Please turn off all cell phones."
Everyone: *Puts cell phone on silent*

I n 1905, the first nickelodeon opened in Columbus, Ohio. (No, not the TV channel with lots of slime, a theater!) Crowds of several hundred people paid 5¢ each to see a movie. (Get it? A *nickel*-odeon?). It was a small but transformative start to the new way Americans created and consumed media. Collective audiences could now consume moving pictures instead of stationary images only being available to individuals in their local newspapers and magazines. Here's an actual photograph of the inside of the theater:

INT. RIOR OF FIRST NICKELODEON IN THE STATES.

Image Source: PA Book Library and Pittsburgh Post Gazette

What strikes me when I see that image is just how similar the setup is to a modern-day movie theater. The only thing missing is maybe a slightly larger screen and some spine-tingling speakers!

But let's back up a bit from the nostalgia, the soft drinks, and the overly buttered popcorn (yum), and think about what a theater means in terms of content, creation, and access.

Let's take a positive twist on things first:

Take 1 | The Movie Theater Experience

- Immersive experiences expose audiences to new worlds and perspectives in a relatively short period of time.
- Films highlight the expertise of certain individuals.
- Compelling narratives captivate audiences and prompt further discussion and deconstruction.

However, let's remind ourselves that catching that early matinee or late-night premiere has some pretty severe limitations:

Take 2 | The Movie Theater Experience

- The owner or outside studio decides what to show or feature. This means that certain narratives or perspectives are prioritized over others.
- Movies are only available at a predetermined schedule with no stopping.
- Movies are mono-lingual (no subtitles).
- Movie are only shown at the theater (specific locations).

So, how does the movie theater appear in our classrooms?

The Movie Theater Experience

- Lessons are centered on lectures, with little to no time for processing information.
- The teacher determines what skills and content are considered valuable and/or normed.
- Lessons are only available at school, in-person, with little to no change of schedule or pacing, and in a single language.

Let's break each of these down, point by point.

Plot Point

PLOT POINT 1: Direct Instruction Is at the Heart of the Movie Theater Model. Its Results Are Mixed.

There is a powerful precedent for direct instruction that spans literally thousands of years. Confucius and Aristotle both taught via lecture, for instance.

For many teachers today, direct instruction is a "default" go-to when introducing material. Some teaching models, such as the gradual release "I Do, We Do, You Do," embrace it wholeheartedly. Others, like PBL (project-based learning) or Inquiry Learning—not so much.

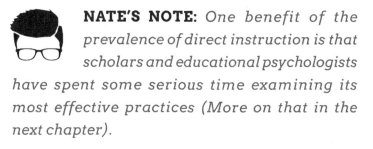

NATE'S NOTE: *One benefit of the prevalence of direct instruction is that scholars and educational psychologists have spent some serious time examining its most effective practices (More on that in the next chapter).*

Most critics point to a few harmful implications of direct instruction:

- The teacher is the commander of knowledge and, by extension, performs the "intellectual weightlifting" of the classroom.

- Students are often viewed as "empty vessels" whose experiences matter less than the teacher's.

- Direct instruction, therefore, emphasizes transmission of knowledge over processing, deconstruction, and meaningful connection-making.

This mini-lesson from my World Geography class reflects these drawbacks pretty accurately:

Lesson available here: tinyurl.com/ridgenationstate

The goal of this mini-lesson was for students to explain the difference between a *nation* and a *state*. The setup was pretty simple: ten minutes of lecture and an exit ticket afterward. I thought the mini-lesson went great, and my students had learned.

But a week later, a short assessment proved me wrong. Only about 60% of students were able to explain the difference between the two terms. What happened?

Let's use our Movie Theater Model as a metaphor for this scenario. First, our characters: I was the theater, and my students were the audience. And the setting: I screened the film *What a Nation Is Versus a State* for them. But why did the film flop?

NATE'S NOTE: *Fellow social studies educator, Steve Heimler, has some great advice on when the right times are for lectures. Read on!*

Some outside scholarship gives us one answer. A recent study (Deslauriers et al. 2019, 19251–19257) compared students' self-perception of learning in two different groups. In the study, two groups experienced the same material: one through "active learning" (cooperative learning, non-teacher centered), and a second group through "passive instruction" (lecture-based, teacher-centered). As expected, researchers found that the passive-learning group learned less than their active-learning counterparts (similar to the students who did my mini-lesson).

But here's where their findings get weird. The active-learning group, despite performing better when assessed, actually believed **they learned less.** The students in the lectures did worse but perceived **they learned more than they had.** "This suggests," they write, "that attempts to evaluate instruction based on students' perceptions of learning could inadvertently promote inferior (passive) pedagogical methods" (2019).

For me, this hits home for two reasons. First, this study makes a lot of sense when I hear students say, "just tell me what I need to know for the test." They understandably, but mistakenly, believe that a lecture results in **meaningful** learning simply because it's so direct. In reality, achieving true understanding takes much more than just a ten-minute lecture, like in my example. Exposure doesn't equate to actual understanding.

> **NATE'S NOTE:** *I've seen "exposure ≠ learning" phenomena show up in my classroom. For example, I've made study guides in a worksheet format for students to answer question-by-question but found them ineffective. Have you found similar trends in your classroom?*

Second, this study helps explain the persistence of direct instruction. It makes students, administrators, and other stakeholders *feel* like students are learning simply because it's visible. The researchers actually reference this phenomenon in their findings. "[Our results] suggest," they write, "that attempts to evaluate instruction based on students' perceptions of learning could inadvertently promote inferior (passive) pedagogical methods" (2019).

> **NATE'S NOTE:** *Got a feeling of, "Wait, so should I talk in front of my classroom at all?" Don't worry. The answer is absolutely yes! You're the expert on your students, and every classroom's needs are different. What we want to avoid are the extremes: all lecture on one side, no guidance on the other.*

So let's return to that Movie Theater Model and add a qualifier:

The Movie Theater Experience

 Lessons are centered on lectures, with little to no time for processing information (but *exposure to knowledge doesn't equate to* _meaningful_ *learning*).

You probably notice the word "meaningful" has been emphasized. We'll get more into this in the next chapter when we explore how to modify and maximize our uses of the Movie Theater Model.

Plot ⮂ Point

PLOT POINT 2: There Are Far-Reaching Consequences When Teachers Become the Singular Voice of the Classroom.

Study after study has shown that there is no single larger influence in a classroom than a teacher (Cantrell and Kane 2013; Chetty et al. 2014; Rockoff et al., 2011). We hold a lot of power in the lives of our students! But as a famous comic book character once said, "With great power comes great responsibility." We have a responsibility to empower all of our students—even (and especially!) the ones who aren't like us.

Hollywood has long struggled to do this. Movies don't do a very good job of representing and complicating the lives of marginalized groups. Although attitudes towards inclusiveness have waxed and waned over time, white, male, cisgendered perspectives in media continue to dominate at the cost of black and brown voices, religious minorities, and individuals in LGBTQIA+ communities.

For example, a 2021 study by the USC Annenberg Inclusion Initiative, called "Missing & Maligned: The Reality of Muslims in Popular Global Movies," found the following when they studied 200 popular movies from 2017–2019:

- 90.5% of these films did not feature a single Muslim speaking character.

- One film had a Muslim woman in a lead role; five films had a Muslim man in a lead role.

- There was only "one fleeting portrayal of a Muslim character that occurred in a US setting."

- Only one Muslim man out of 8,965 characters was LGBTQ, and only one was shown with a disability.

This study highlights the same struggle in classrooms throughout the United States (2021). Ultimately, as teachers, we have the power and responsibility to change the dynamics of misrepresentation, marginalization, and minimization. We can do this in our schools and classrooms—no matter the grade, subject, or locale. **Modifying or moving away from the Movie Theater Model is a small yet significant step toward celebrating our students' voices and experiences.**

I've taught high school social studies for eight years now, and I've come to a tough conclusion: My teaching has focused too much on myself.

My old approach to teaching the Civil Rights Movement in my Dual Credit US History Course serves as a good yet painful example of this. I attempted to teach the entirety of the movement with a couple of mini-lessons and some processing activities—and in just two days!

The results were disastrous. I had done students a triple disservice:

1. I taught the civil rights movement superficially.

2. My students did not achieve much meaningful learning on a very timely, relevant, and important topic.

3. But most crucially, *I silenced my students' struggles for racial and socio-political equality by teaching through my own worldview.*

So this past year (2021), I decided to completely reteach civil rights—shifting away from the Movie Theater Model—and the results were vastly different.

- Students could voice their own interpretations of the Civil Rights Movement while being pushed to challenge common misconceptions.

■ Students could now collaborate and have input on topics ranging from Choose-Your-Journey Stories to role-play scenarios.

Check it out below!

Link: tinyurl.com/civilrightsridge

My first attempt at teaching the Civil Rights Movement highlighted the real price of the Movie Theater Model—a sort of hidden fee, if you will. Direct instruction silenced the perspectives of my students.

Economists call this "opportunity cost," the loss incurred when one opportunity is pursued over another.

To make this easier to understand, imagine you own a drive-in theater. Two new superhero movies have just come out—one from Marvel and one from DC. You only have one time slot open for the evening before a batch of bad weather arrives and only one large screen. You can only pick one movie to play. Which do you choose?

No matter your loyalties to Marvel or DC, **the actual answer is that it doesn't matter.** You'll pay a cost no matter what you pick. The opportunity cost is the lost chance to play the other film.

You can probably figure out how this applies to our classrooms pretty quickly. Teachers only have limited resources (time, money, sanity, etc.) to teach a vast amount of standards, concepts, and skills. Across the entire year, we're constantly forced to make difficult decisions about **what to teach** at the cost of something else.

But what the Movie Theater Model helps us understand is that opportunity cost applies to **how we teach**, too. When we do too much direct instruction or a teacher-centric pedagogy, it comes at the cost of student voices or other outside perspectives. Put another way, if we decide to teach through a lecture, we've made a choice to value our voice over others. That's a big call to make, even if it feels like it might be the right one.

Once again, let's return to that Movie Theater Model infographic and add another qualifier:

The Movie Theater Experience

- Lessons are centered on lectures, with little to no time for processing information (but *exposure to knowledge doesn't equate to meaningful learning*).

- The teacher determines what skills and content are considered valuable and/or normed (but *featuring the teacher's voice, even if it's the right call, can come at the cost of valuable perspectives, especially our students'*).

Plot ⮂ Point

PLOT POINT 3: The Traditional Stance that Learning Is or Should Be Limited to What Happens within the Walls of Our Classrooms Is Archaic and Harmful.

The last tenet of the Movie Theater Model is its stance toward the learner's access to relevant resources, knowledge, or skills. Again, it helps to think first about the metaphor of movie theaters rather than our classrooms. When it comes down to it, it doesn't take long to realize that the act of "going to the movies" is a pretty restrictive activity.

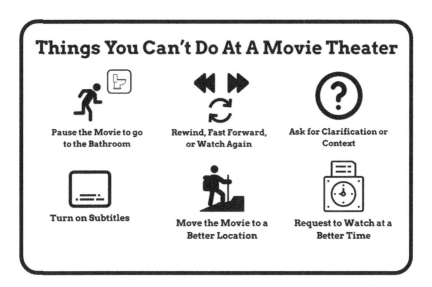

Things You Can't Do At A Movie Theater

Pause the Movie to go to the Bathroom

Rewind, Fast Forward, or Watch Again

Ask for Clarification or Context

Turn on Subtitles

Move the Movie to a Better Location

Request to Watch at a Better Time

For teachers, this is where movie theaters could use some UDL, or Universal Design for Learning, to help open up access.

If you're new to this term, UDL is a philosophical framework developed by an organization called CAST. Broadly speaking, the ideas in UDL originated in architecture, where experts were trying to create more accessible buildings. Theorists and practitioners in education then applied the same ideas to create the framework we have today.

You can find the guidelines and detailed descriptions of each checkpoint at udlguidelines.cast.org.

Here are CAST's UDL guidelines in full:

The Universal Design for Learning Guidelines

Universal Design for Learning is a framework to improve and optimize teaching and learning for all people based on scientific insights into how humans learn. Learn more at **udlguidelines.cast.org**.

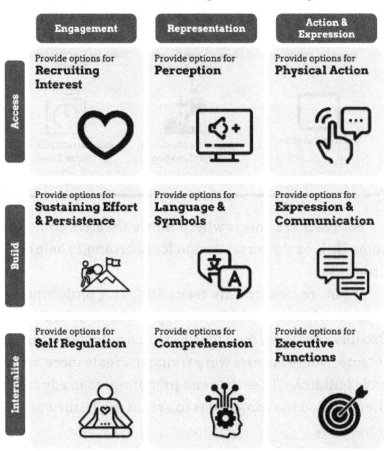

	Engagement	Representation	Action & Expression
Access	Provide options for **Recruiting Interest**	Provide options for **Perception**	Provide options for **Physical Action**
Build	Provide options for **Sustaining Effort & Persistence**	Provide options for **Language & Symbols**	Provide options for **Expression & Communication**
Internalize	Provide options for **Self Regulation**	Provide options for **Comprehension**	Provide options for **Executive Functions**

CAST (2018). Universal design for learning guidelines version 2.2 [graphic organizer]. Wakefield, MA: Author.

To keep things simple, we're going to focus on the three main columns and summarize them like this: **we, as teachers, need to help provide students with varied ways to engage with, represent, and express their content knowledge**. If we think back to the limitations of the Movie Theater Model style of direct instruction, we can immediately see how UDL provides a useful remedy.

Theory is all well and good, but is UDL worth it? In my opinion, it's an unequivocal yes, but here's a sample of what researchers find about UDL too:

- "UDL-based instruction has the potential to **increase engagement** and access to general education curriculum for students with disabilities, and **improve students' academic and social outcomes.**"(Ok et al. 2017)

- "UDL is an effective teaching methodology for improving the learning process **for all students.**"(Capp 2017)

- "UDL is an efficient approach for designing flexible learning environments and accessible content. Such designs can match a wide mix of learner needs, abilities, background knowledge, educational experience, and cultural differences." (Al-Azawei, Serenelli, and Lundqvist 2016)

If you're still not convinced about the need for UDL, I would argue that a more recent event should motivate us more than anything: COVID-19.

NATE'S NOTE: *Teachers can't be responsible for implementing UDL alone. Administrators, staff, families, and local organizations need to be involved in supporting all students' equitable access to learning.*

COVID-19 was (and still is, as of 2022) the greatest force to ever hit schools across the United States in recent times. It's really important to understand that COVID challenged the US education system universally, yet its impacts were vastly dependent upon socio-economic, ethnic, political, and geographical circumstances. Schools that stayed open, closed, or went to alternative systems such as hybrid models all faced unique demands. However, the institutions, students, educators, and families most affected were communities of color and those lacking financial privilege. Just in my own state of Indiana, pre-pandemic data about internet and computer access didn't leave us much to suspect whom COVID hurt most (Weddle 2020). In 2018:

- 10% of Indiana children did not have a computer or broadband internet.
- 15% of Indiana Latinx students did not have a computer or broadband internet.
- 21% of Indiana black students did not have a computer or broadband internet.
- 50% to 75% of children in Indianapolis' poorest neighborhoods, the Eastside and Northside, did not have a computer or broadband internet.

NATE'S NOTE: *It's crucial to know your own students' access to devices and broadband. If your school or district doesn't know, data is generally available via your state's Department of Education or through other local studies. You can also try a quick student survey at the beginning of the year for specific data for your class.*

That same universal yet unequal impact of COVID hit teachers, too. We were all challenged to adopt new classroom setups, assessments, and communication platforms. Overall, COVID made the difficult work that *every* teacher does just that much harder.

Where COVID affected teachers unequally was in access to edtech, administrative support, and professional development. Individuals with those advantages found more success, while those without suffered.

So what should we take from teaching in COVID? Access matters.

What we can and should capitalize on from COVID as an educational system is a chance, likely the greatest chance we've ever had, to rethink our institutional and instructional practices that consistently prove to be barriers to success. Metaphorically speaking, it's time to renovate or move past our restrictive movie theaters.

Let's make one final modification to our infographic:

The Movie Theater Experience

🎥 Lessons are centered on lectures, with little to no time for processing information (but *exposure to knowledge doesn't equate to meaningful learning*).

🎥 The teacher determines what skills and content are considered valuable and/or normed (but *featuring the teacher's voice, even if it's the right call, can come at the cost of valuable perspectives, especially our students'*).

🎥 Lessons are only available at school, in-person, with little to no change of schedule or pacing, and in a single language (but *this framework of access needs to be modified*).

So, in movie theater moments, how can we better create meaningful learning? How can we better feature student voices, agency, and perspectives? How can we better open up access?

Let's head to the next chapter, "The Sequel," to find out.

CHAPTER TWO

The Sequel: Getting the Most from Movie Theater Moments

Every Horror Movie:
"Let's split up to cover more ground."

There are some movies that you just *have* to see in theaters, right? Think back. What was a film that you were glad to see in that setting? I'll always remember three films in particular that I saw in theaters, for very different reasons.

The first was a live-action remake of *101 Dalmatians*, one of the first films I remember seeing in my life. I was four or five at the time, and it scared me to death. I was so frightened by it that I made my mom (bless her) walk out of the theater with me after thirty minutes, a fact made all the more funny that I now own a dalmatian named Perdita.

The second film I remember was when I was really little, a 4D immersive *A Bug's Life* film in Walt Disney World. The 4D part came with the added effects, like wind during blustery scenes and humidity underground. The stinkbug parts, well, you can likely surmise how that went.

My last memorable movie in theaters was actually my first IMAX movie—*Avatar*. (No, not the *Last Airbender* one.) I was blown away by the optics and auditory experience. Even though it wasn't the greatest narrative in the world, the sheer immersiveness of the experience was awesome. Something about the IMAX setup—that wraparound screen, surround sound, great visuals—made it worth it.

So why do some movies, like those above, stick with us? What about these movies made them memorable? With streaming services like Netflix and Amazon Prime Video, we can watch movies on our sofas in our living rooms. Often, we pay a fraction of the cost to do so. Yet we still go to movie theaters—and pay extra to do so—even with their limitations and inflexibilities. We still do it. Is the movie theater dead? Not at all! In fact, it still has its strengths in certain situations. The classroom Movie Theater Model is very much the same.

This chapter is focused on how we can maximize or modify the Movie Theater Model in our classrooms to have the best outcomes for student learning. You'll see that there's A LOT of practical advice here that ties into the more theoretical things we just discussed in Chapter 1. Even if the examples don't perfectly fit your content area or grade level, you can modify many of them to meet your needs. You'll also see no-tech, low-tech, and high-tech strategies from other educators across the world that you can modify many of them to meet your needs.

Before we begin, I want to make two very important points about edtech and teaching:

POINT 1: Solid, evidence-based practices (direct instruction or otherwise) should always be prioritized over the desire to use a new app or edtech setup. Said simply, pedagogy over products.

Good instruction, not the newest apps, has the most powerful impact on student learning. This means that we keep doing the things that good teachers do:

Pedagogy Over Products

Students are scaffolded and supported at various levels.

Student choice is integrated and offered.

Time is provided for metacognitive practice.

Models for process & product are accessible.

Connections are made to the the real-world and prior learning.

Timely & relevant feedback helps personalize learning.

Information is "chunked" into short, meaningful segments.

Information is accessible for families.

Learning has measurable outcomes & can be assessed.

POINT 2: Choosing not to integrate edtech in some capacity in your classroom will come at the cost of student learning and preparedness for living and working in a modern world.

A 2017 report by Burning Glass Technologies, which analyzes market and employment trends, argues that "the number of jobs with digital skill requirements is growing faster, and the jobs pay more (17% on average) and offer greater opportunity for career advancement than jobs without those requirements." Stated more simply, **students need to start developing their digital toolkits alongside their academic, social-emotional, and cognitive ones.**

In this chapter, you'll find six ways to change the direct instruction Movie Theater Model to improve student learning and get results. Each one contains tips, tools, and things you can try yourself.

With all that said, let's do it!

NATE'S NOTE: *Want to know more about where to get started with edtech in your classroom? Check out a free e-book here:*

tinyurl.com/edtechebook

As we said earlier, despite the weaknesses in the Movie Theater Model, there's still a place for parts of direct instruction in today's classroom, including lectures. The question is, when should we use it? For more on that, I asked Steve Heimler, a fellow history teacher and host of the popular YouTube channel, Heimler's History, to give us some guidance.

Plot ⤭ Twist

PLOT TWIST 1: Use Lectures Strategically.

Educator  Voice

STEVE HEIMLER
@HeimlersHistory

When's the right time to lecture? Well, earlier, Nate referenced the truism that the person who does the thinking does the learning, but I would add a second strand to the proposition: the person that does the feeling also does the learning, and lecturing can be an exacting tool for arousing the emotions of our students.

Lecturing has fallen on hard times not because it is ineffective as a tool for learning but because of the preponderance of bad lecturing. We cannot blame a dulled knife when it doesn't cut. A skilled surgeon with a dull scalpel will do a great deal of damage, despite his or her skills. The effectiveness of a tool must be judged by its proper use, not by its improper use.

We are all familiar with the improper use of the lecture, namely, as an expedient for content delivery: *"The Mongol Empire was the largest land-based empire in history, bigger than the Greeks, bigger than the Romans. The way the Mongols achieved this was through innovative military techniques and diplomacy with conquered peoples."* In this way, the teacher's lecture is nothing more than a verbalized version of a textbook.

The problems with this method are legion, but the crux of the matter is this: oral communication is not a medium that helps students to ingest complex, didactic propositions. In fact, books are the medium best suited for that. On a page, theses and evidence can be stacked one upon another, and the learner can take all the time he or she needs to metabolize the arguments. With oral communication, words stream into the ear, not the eye, and complexity is often lost in the process.

So then, what is a lecture good for? A lecture is a tool designed to awaken the imagination of your students to a world that would otherwise remain hidden from them. A lecture should be less like a verbalized textbook passage and more like a walk through the woods when, all of the sudden, your breath is taken away because, in the clearing ahead, you see fairies dancing around a unicorn stamping its hooves. You pause, catch your breath, and behold this unguessed wonder. In that moment, it is the emotions by which we learn, not the rational structures of the mind.

All things being equal, students should always do the work of learning themselves, for the mind always embraces the conclusions to which it comes on its own. However, there are times when our students need a guide to help them see something which is otherwise unseeable by their own lights. The main way we, as teachers, do that is by casting our lectures in the form of a narrative, the most basic structure of which is tension and release.

If we are able to learn from storytellers how to build tension, which in a story is fundamentally an affair of the emotions, then our audience will demand its resolution, for the human being cannot long endure unresolved tension. Of course, the methods for building tension are more than I could number here: begin with misconceptions, demonstrate that everything they think they know about X is wrong, tell a proper story in which you bring the students to the climax of the plot and then leave them dangling on the precipice while you give them the information they need. All of these methods work well for inducing emotional involvement in a student, and generally speaking, whatever information a lecturer drops into that tension will be remembered. After all, stories are easy to remember because they awaken our imaginations.

Lecturing is a tool best employed for awakening the imaginations of our students so that they may experience a world otherwise shut to them. Therefore, in practice, this means that I only give a proper lecture on a handful of occasions during the year. And the main criterion by which I make that decision is this: does this topic make me come alive? If so, there is no way a lecture like that will put students to sleep.

Plot ⤸ Twist

PLOT TWIST 2: Record Your Direct Instruction (If Possible).

As frustrating as sitting on Zoom through the pandemic was, there's one skill we improved a lot: being on video! While it isn't always practical or possible, the occasional recording has silver linings:

1. **It helps students who need extra support.** Studies find that "lecture recordings are an effective way to support students disclosing dyslexia and other SpLDs [Special Learning Disabilities], and have a role to play in inclusive curricula" (Nightingale et al. 2019).

2. **Once made, you get a recording you can use forever with unlimited use.** Although making a video at first is an investment, I found that by the first moment of a student being absent or asking, "wait, what did we learn last class?" the time invested had paid for itself.

NATES NOTE: *Looking for a Flipped Classroom model? Look ahead to Chapter 5, where we'll explore it and an upgraded version called "Cloning."*

If you're brand new to putting yourself in front of a camera and speaking, it can be slightly nerve-wracking. But don't worry! Here are a few things to keep in mind to help get you started:

Making Your First Recording

Breathe.
You can always
re-record or make
edits later.

Look at the
camera, not the
screen. Eye
contact matters.

Speak up!
Be clear and loud
enough to be easily
understood.

Use any visuals
you can (slides,
pictures, etc.) to
help add variety.

Lights up!
Make sure your
face is well-lit and
not in the dark.

Store your files on
the cloud, such as
YouTube or
Google Drive.

Once your recording is made, it's as simple as making it available to students the best way you see fit. Upload your video to Google Drive, YouTube, or anyplace else that lets you host and share videos. Get a link and make sure the sharing settings allow your students to view it. Then, distribute it to students. Here are some easy ways to share your videos with students:

- Share the link in an announcement or assignment in your learning management system (like Google Classroom, Canvas, or Schoology).

- Create a simple website using something like Google Sites or Microsoft Sway. Add your videos to it and share the website link with your students.

- Record your videos directly to Flipgrid (flipgrid. com), creating a topic called "5th Grade ELA Videos" or "Algebra II Videos." Set the topic so videos display automatically in that topic after recording. Then, share a link to the topic with your students.

- Gather links to your videos—and even videos created by others—in a Wakelet collection (wakelet.com), YouTube playlist, or Pinterest board.

If you're well-versed in creating recordings, you might be ready to revamp and redesign the video-making experience to have the greatest impact on student learning. If you want to level up, a *Journal of Learning Design* study (Thomson, Bridgstock, and Willems 2014) recommends that videos:

1. **Are planned, scripted, and prepared with resources beforehand,** such as images or models. You want to focus on the content of your presentation, not "housekeeping" material that is unrelated to the topic at hand. If you don't like crafting a word-for-word script, a series of bullet points is a good half-step.

2. **Provide context and purpose.** Provide any background info needed, and be upfront with viewers about what to expect.

3. **Reveal or tell a story.** Think of video as "visual storytelling." Back up your narratives with images. Note: this is not carte blanche permission to PowerPoint viewers to death. Visual elements have to be used purposefully.

4. **Are kept as short as possible.** The average YouTube video is four minutes and twelve seconds long, and 40% are watched on mobile devices. Videos need to get to the point quickly. If you have multiple concepts to explain, break them into separate videos.

5. **Are presented authentically**. Viewers want to hear your voice. They want your personality to shine through. That kind of performance and confidence takes time to develop. Your viewers—your students!—should feel like you're talking just to them, one-on-one.

In particular, I love #s 3 and 5. I've always believed that, ultimately, a persuasive video takes an audience captive and shares a relatable voice or message. Movies are much the same. So if you're not sure where to start with upping your video skills, start with **an engaging story first**. The rest will come with practice and time.

 NATE'S NOTE: *There is a vast amount of video already available online through YouTube, Khan Academy, Vimeo, and other sites, so it may be well-worth saving yourself some time and finding something already made. For more info, see this Wakelet collection of favorite sites for different content areas and ages, curated by other teachers and me.*

bit.ly/youtuberidge

Looking for some movie-making tech? There are many, many options, but here are my three favorites:

www.flipgrid.com

If you're not familiar with Flipgrid, it's one of the most popular—and powerful—edtech apps on the market. On its face, it's a free video response/assessment platform. But it's so much more. It includes a "Shorts" feature where teachers record videos for direct instruction. Then, they can share those videos directly with students, parents, or anyone. Although a Shorts video can only be 10 minutes long, Flipgrid is free and easy to use, share, and edit. Plus, Flipgrid stores your videos on its servers, so no hard drive or cloud storage is required!

Maryland teacher Stacey Roshan demonstrates how to make classroom magic with Flipgrid's Shorts camera. Check out the video here:

bit.ly/learnflipgridcamera

NATE'S NOTE: *if you're interested in using Flipgrid more in your classroom, Stacey Roshan and I collaborated on an e-book for asynchronous, flipped, and remote classroom instruction. There's a full page*

 *dedicated to walkthroughs, examples, and samples of how to use Flipgrid meaningfully. Find it here:*

bit.ly/flippedebook

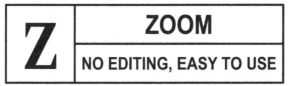

www.zoom.com

Zoom might seem like a surprise to add to a list of screencast apps. I recommend it because of many educators' familiarity with it after COVID-19 remote learning. Plus, it's easy to use. Simply start a meeting alone, then hit record! The only downside to Zoom is that you'll have to edit videos separately (if that's something you're interested in). You'll also need to store finished videos on your own device or somewhere in the cloud. One nice positive is that it transcribes any speech for later use.

S	**STREAMLABS**
	COMPLEX, NO TIME LIMIT, CUSTOMIZABLE, FREE

www.streamlabs.com

Streamlabs is meant for streaming video games and other content to platforms like Twitch and YouTube, but I love its recording feature because I can customize the video setup and screencast appearance for a more per-

sonalized touch. It is pretty complex, though. If you'd like to try it, I recommend checking out this video where I cover setup and design:

bit.ly/3zf9fBy

Plot ⤨ Twist

PLOT TWIST 3: Provide Support During Direct Instruction.

There's nothing more frustrating than watching a movie and being lost. If we can do direct instruction well in the classroom, we can spare students from that same experience and save instructional time by keeping everyone on script.

Research has shown that providing note outlines or handouts of slides is an effective learning practice. One *Applied Cognitive Psychology* study (Marsh and Sink 2010) found that "having access to handouts of the slides during lecture was associated with a number of benefits: less note-taking [...] less time needed to prepare for a final test ... and better performance on the final test. Overall, receiving handouts before lecture helped efficient encoding of the lecture."

Strategy: Varied Note Options During Lectures

Speaking of scripts, it may actually save time and increase student success when all scripts aren't the same.

I always provide students with a variety of options to take notes in my class during my mini-lessons. I'll vary these options over time depending on student readiness and my own preferences.

Fill-In-The-Blank	Exactly what it sounds like! Perfect for students who need the extra support.	bit.ly/3k5mvnO
Open-Ended	Gives students a scaffold to construct their notes, but leaves the content up to them.	bit.ly/3yOmCsf

Collaborative Notes	There are so many fun variations of collaborative notes, and I've named a few I've used after some recognizable movie titles. Check out the link!	bit.ly/ridgenotes
Independent Note-Taking	A harder option for students, and only when they've mastered note-taking skills.	
Sketchnotes	For students who are more visual or artistically inclined, this is a wonderful, though more time-consuming, choice. If you want to get students started with sketchnoting, Jen Giffen (@VirtualGiff) is a great resource.	bit.ly/2UXBcP2

As a high school teacher, I provide fill-in-the-blank notes (the easiest option) for the first part of the semester. As time goes on and note-taking skills improve, I remove that option. If you want your students to move to more independent note-taking, don't remove options and just expect success. Students need support, guidance, and practice to develop. We'll talk about making embedded skills like note-taking more visible within your classroom in Chapter 5.

Strategy: Scaffold Online Readings

Direct instruction isn't always teacher-led. It also encompasses a wide variety of other resources like textbooks, articles, and websites. I've felt text resources rarely meet the needs of students. Maybe the vocab inside is a bit lacking or too hard, or the topic needs some updates or extra detail.

One way to address this is to find or adapt a source into a more supportive digital format. Here are some of my favorite apps that can help:

App: Insert Learning

Insert Learning is an amazing way to provide scaffolding with ease in just a few minutes (think like an Edpuzzle for everything but video), and collect student data for later analysis. Check it out here: www.insertlearning.com.

App: Immersive Reader

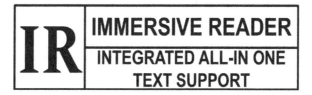

Immersive Reader is a Microsoft-based reading support tool with built-in translation, visual dictionaries, pronunciation help, plus much more. It's integrated into many apps out there, such as the Microsoft Edge browser, Flipgrid, PearDeck, and Wonderopolis. There's also a Google Chrome add-on available here: bit.ly/ImmersiveChrome

App: Tween Tribune

The Smithsonian's free Tween Tribune site makes finding a variety of differentiated readings a snap. Simply click the different Lexile Levels below an article to instantly scaffold a text for a variety of readers. Find it here: www.tweentribune.com

Plot ⤬ Twist

PLOT TWIST 4: Set Time for Meaningful Processing & Retrieval.

Pretty much anyone can relate to a trip to the movies that felt like a waste. You might have been let down by the hype of a trailer. You might have spent way too much on tickets. All the seats might have been sold out.

But there's something else that can ruin a film: a plot that doesn't make sense or that doesn't allow viewers to make sense of it. The same is true for direct instruction in our classrooms.

Direct instruction has to be paired with opportunities for students to understand what they've learned, as well as to use it later. I'll refer to this phenomenon as "processing" and "retrieval," but you've likely heard similar terms in your ed psych background (rehearsal, elaboration, etc.). Just to get us all on the same page, though, let's take a brief trip down memory lane (pun very intended) and check out this information processing model for some quick reference (Atkinson and Shiffrin 1968).

The Information Processing Model

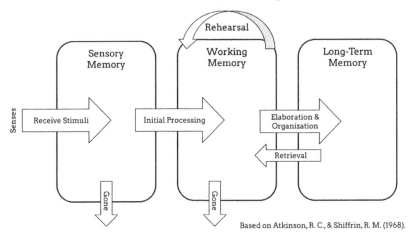

Based on Atkinson, R. C., & Shiffrin, R. M. (1968).

What we're really concerned with here are the two rightmost arrows. We want to make sure that students have time to first meaningfully **process** what they've learned (referred to on the model as elaboration and organization) and then to practice **retrieving** the information for later use. It's pretty hard for me to underscore just how important the link is between these elements. Not pairing direct instruction with processing and retrieval is like ending a movie without a plot resolution.

For some help on this, I asked Patrice Bain, co-author of *Powerful Teaching* (2019), to share her journey toward a more retrieval-focused classroom:

Educator 📢 Voice

PATRICE BAIN
@ PatriceBain1

I was a teacher who used the Movie Theater Model in my middle school world history classroom. In fact, I likened my curriculum to the movies. My classes were filled with the stories of heroes, villains, wars, love stories, and mysteries. Hollywood had nothing over me. I held center stage and thought many of my direct-instruction productions were Academy Award-worthy (humbly speaking, of course). Processing the information? Who had time for that? I had another civilization to cover! The majority of my students turned in homework and received high scores on tests. Yet, I began to see that my students were not retaining any of the grandeur I worked so hard to present. When asking a question from a previous lesson, blank stares became my feedback. I realized that although my students seemed to be engaged in class, they had "mastered homework" (read a question, looked up the answer, wrote it down, repeat) and crammed for tests. Thus, some received high grades. So why the blank stares and lack of knowledge retention?

It was around this time (clear back in 2006!) that two cognitive scientists, Dr. Henry Roediger and Dr. Mark McDaniel, came up with the novel idea of studying how students learn in an authentic classroom. (Previously, most studies had been conducted at colleges, in laboratories, with college students.) The classroom where the research began was mine. Cognitive scientist Dr. Pooja Agarwal, one of Roediger's and McDaniel's colleagues, came and worked with me daily. Our first year of research concentrated on retrieval. I knew my teaching trajectory was taking a different route. As Dr. Agarwal stated, "Too often we concentrate on getting information into our students' heads. What if, instead, we focused on pulling information out?" Retrieval became the missing link. I developed strategies based on the idea of pulling information out and having students retrieve it. Rather than assigning mindless homework, I began giving mini-quizzes the following day. Whatever we had discussed (and what I wanted my students to remember) became mini-quiz questions. To the students, my questions may have seemed random. To me, they were strategic and focused. Because these five-question mini-quizzes became an everyday occurrence, I noticed my students began listening differently in class. I developed more retrieval strategies. I explained why retrieval was vital. The blank stares began to disappear. Our class discussions became lively, and essays written by eleven-year-olds were worthy of AP exams. Best yet? This newfound success was felt by all of my students.

As the research continued in my classroom, we began looking at other principles of the science of learning. Spacing, described as intentional retrieval over time, became an area of focus. Before beginning a new unit of study, I began to look at the unit's end products. What did I most want my students to retain? These items became my target for retrieval. I taught my students why we went over information, and we retrieved information from previous lessons. Weaving the information together became my dance. My students had become critical thinkers and successful writers of thought-provoking essays.

And yet, there was one more principle of the science of learning. It's a "Power Tool" highlighted in the book *Powerful Teaching*, which I co-authored with Pooja Agarwal. This principle, metacognition, played a leading role in my class. It can be defined as "thinking about thinking." What I realized is that this metacognition is often what separates those who scored well from those who didn't. Each year I asked my new students, "Have you ever studied hard for a test and didn't do well?" Year after year, about 98% would say yes. I explained metacognition to my students. It's the ability to differentiate what we know from what we don't. Too often, students tend to study what they already know. They get so discouraged because, despite studying hard, they do not score well on tests. Developing strategies that enabled student success became my mission. (You can find and download these strategies at powerfulteaching.org/resources.)

My students continued to score high on exams, but it wasn't because of cramming the night before. Blank stares were replaced by lively discussions. Frequent emails from those I had taught years earlier exclaimed how what they learned (and retained) in 6th grade was helping them in college.

Much has become known since those early days of research in authentic classrooms. More and more, cognitive science and the science of learning have become widespread. Teachers are realizing the impact of these "Power Tools": retrieval, spacing, and metacognition, along with other key concepts like working memory and cognitive load. The success stories and happy endings—which we adore in the movies—are becoming the epics of our classrooms.

Here are 20 strategies I use with my students to help them meaningfully process direct instruction, as well as retrieve it later. None of them requires tech of any kind. They are multi-modal and work with any subject area. They only take fifteen minutes or less. Note: if you're trying these for the first time in your class, you'll need to offer support and scaffolding until students can do them independently.

20 Meaningful Processing/Retrieval Strategies for Students

1) Flyswatter

Using 3x5 cards, have students write terms/definitions and then "swat" them when a peer reads the definition/term.

2) Record Yourself

Have students recap material on video or audio. Have them listen and make revisions.

3) Memory

Using 3x5 cards, students play the game Memory with relevant vocab.

4) Study Guide Highlight

Instead of answering a study guide for a test, have students go through and highlight questions you can't immediately answer.

5) Matching

Using 3x5 cards, have students play Memory but with the cards all facing upward so they can sort them.

6) Script It

Have students create a quick script for a movie/play about a topic/event/skill.

7) Draw It!

Have students draw a picture of a complicated story, an indepth mini-lesson, or a tough vocab word.

8) Objective Flip

Have students take the objectives from a mini-lesson and flip them into questions that they have to answer.

9) Make An Infographic

Infographics use charts, pictures, and text to convey information. Have students make one!

10) Thirty-Second Summary

Have students summarize an event, vocab word, etc. in exactly thirty seconds. They'll likely find you have more time than they need, but they'll be forced to add on details and examples to fill the entire thirty seconds.

20 Meaningful Processing/Retrieval Strategies for Students

11) Make A Vocab Puzzle

Have students make a vocab puzzle. Check out Chapter 4 to see how!

12) Tweet It

Have students explain a complicated issue in 140 characters or less while still including all relevant details.

13) Quiz A Friend

Have students quiz a peer on what they just learned about.

14) 360 No-Scope

In the middle of direct instruction, black out your presentation screen. Then, have students (without looking at their notes) write or talk with a peer about what they just learned.

15) Make A Comic

Have students draw a comic of a complicated story or an in depth mini-lesson.

16) Love.Com

Have students make an online dating profile for a famous person, thing, event, or place. They should include three traits or achievements that people might fall in love with.

17) Beach Ball Quiz

Put tape strips on a beach ball and write questions on them. Have students toss the ball between them. They answer the question their left thumb lands closest to.

18) Make A Haiku

Poetry as a summary tool!
A haiku has:
Five Syllables
Seven Syllables
Five Syllables

20 Meaningful Processing/Retrieval Strategies for Students

19) Fortune Tellers

Like they did in elementary school, have students make a fortune teller with vocab. The "reveal" part of the fortune teller should be the vocab definition, answer, etc.

20) Memes

Have students create memes about a topic, idea, event, etc., that make sense (and are funny).

Want more? Check out dozens more processing and retrieval activities here!

bit.ly/22processing

Plot ⤨ Twist

PLOT TWIST 5: Make it Interactive.

Take a moment and think about a main character in a movie or TV show who had to make a seemingly impossible choice.

You're not sure what they're going to do. The tension seems unbearable. And then they choose. Their path is set.

Take a step back. It's weird, but no matter what *you* thought the character *should* have done, you, the viewer, actually didn't have any influence on the character in the first place. The choice was already filmed and set in stone, right?

What if you *could* change their choice? Or how a scene appeared? The costumes the characters wore? In other words, **what if our movies could be interactive?**

Interactivity is a crucial component of direct instruction because it allows students to engage and retain attention, and it can even be fun. I always try to think about my lessons happening in a children's museum instead of a high-end art gallery. In the first, touch and play are encouraged; in the latter, they're discouraged. Which place do you think most students would like to visit more? Here are some strategies that a few teachers and I love to use.

App: Pear Deck

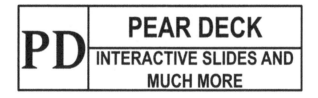

www.PearDeck.com

Pear Deck is one of my favorite edtech apps in the classroom ever and the go-to for thousands of educators around the world. And there's a good reason why: it lets you turn any slide deck (Google Slides or PowerPoint) into an interactive experience of dragging, typing, drawing, and much more.

Remember those processing and retrieval practices we just discussed? Pear Deck lets you build them right in. There are so many potential applications beyond direct instruction, including SEL (social-emotional learning), metacognition, and asynchronous learning.

For the teacher looking to take that first step on how to improve the Movie Theater Model, it's perfect. It also does a great job with diverse representation (which we'll discuss shortly).

Here is a bunch of resources I recommend checking out:

- Try out a Pear Deck session as a student here (Google account required): bit.ly/3BlqYJt

- If you're ready to try it out for yourself as a teacher, check out these videos from Stacey Roshan: bit.ly/SlidesPear and bit.ly/PearDashboard

- Looking for Engagement Ideas? Check out "20 Ways to Use Pear Deck to Engage Students" from educator Matt Miller: DitchThatTextbook.com/peardeck

- Need more guidance? Look at the Pear Deck page on this e-book: bit.ly/flippedebook

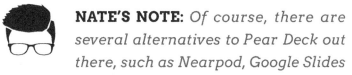 **NATE'S NOTE:** *Of course, there are several alternatives to Pear Deck out there, such as Nearpod, Google Slides Q&A, and others. Pick what works best for your students. I prefer Pear Deck for its versatility, representation, and ease of use.*

Strategy: Do the 2 Step

Still want to make things interactive but with a no-tech twist? Do the "2 Step." **Stop at least after every 2 slides of a presentation or 2 paragraphs of reading to have students do something interactive.** (Rates will vary depending on your students, of course.) It could be chatting with a peer about what they've learned so far, drawing a summary on their notes, or answering a quick question you've pre-planted in the slides. I've found that these occasional pauses sustain interest, add variety, and promote metacognition.

Strategy: Embed Experiences

There's nothing wrong with having a break in your direct instruction for wandering, discovering, and then reconvening. Although I don't want to dive down the rabbit hole of experiential learning just yet, suffice it to say that opportunities for students **to experience something** can mean more than just **us telling it to them.** We'll explore this topic much more in-depth in future chapters, but here are some of my favorite activities to embed inside of direct instruction.

- **StoryMap by KnightLab:** Combines a SlideDeck with maps.
  - Link: storymap.knightlab.com
  - Example: One Perspective on the Persian War: goo.gl/RRSg14
  - Example: A Different Perspective: goo.gl/EB687b

- **Choose Your Own Journey Stories:** Interactive choices meet reading.
  - A Step-By-Step Guide to Make Your Own CYOJS: bit.ly/2zaGjjW
  - Example of Nate's Stories, "A Tiny Dynasty": bit.ly/2u3kcH5

- **Newseum:** Newspaper front pages from around the world.
  - Link: bit.ly/3Bk5Djp

- **Twitter Moments:** Teacher-curated tweets of text, audio, pictures, and videos that can be safely consumed.
  - Nate's Example: bit.ly/2ID9rEH
  - How to Make Your Own Twitter Moment: bit.ly/2J0iUWh

Plot ⤭ Twist

PLOT TWIST 6: Promote Representation.

As we mentioned in the last chapter, Hollywood has had some pretty serious issues with equitable representation across multiple demographic groups. Broadly speaking, our schools have mirrored this trend, too. "Traditional" perspectives (often white, male, heterosexual, cisgender, and ableist) manifest themselves in the curricula we teach, decisions made about school funding, and staff hiring choices.

While there is no single starting point for any educator to begin or continue to enact change, **making changes to how we do direct instruction is certainly a small yet measurable way to do so**. But just to be clear, this means that these efforts:

- Can't be performative or just for the sake of show. It means featuring figures, events, and perspectives with the intention of creating change.

- Have to be long-lasting and deep. Doing a single "Black History unit" or a highlight of "famous female scientists" doesn't cut it.

- Come from a place of understanding, growth, grace, and most importantly, listening.

Victoria Thompson, one of my favorite equity-minded educators out there, is a K-12 education industry executive and former math teacher and STEM coach. She offers these thoughts on creating a more equity-focused educational experience for our students:

Educator  Voice

VICTORIA THOMPSON
@ VictoriaTheTech

When I think about equity in education, my mind immediately goes to the difference between equity and equality. The best way that I differentiate the two is that equality means that we all have a pair of shoes, but equity means that we all have shoes that fit. Equality means that we all get the same of something, while equity means that we individually get what we need in order to be successful.

To think about equity in the classroom, we need to be mindful of implementation. Specifically, how do we want to do this, and how are we doing this for our students? As Nate mentioned, there is not necessarily a single starting point for any educator to begin or enact change. I'd like to also highlight that no matter where you are in your journey, baby steps are still steps. You can start small and still have an immense impact on equity work in your classroom, school, or district.

It all begins with figuring out your "why." Why do you want to create more equitable experiences for your students? For me, my "why" was making sure that students had opportunities for inclusive activities and resources that could help them succeed. When you find your "why," it can also guide you toward figuring out how that relates to your instructional strategies and work within your classroom.

As you ask yourself about your "why," it is also good practice to ask students their "why" but with a twist. Ask for their "why and how." As educators, we only provide one perspective regarding equity; reaching out to our students also gives us their perspective on how the classroom can be a more equitable space. Particularly, why do they come to school each day, and how do they want to use what they learned in school to change the world? You can use these "whys and hows" to help you determine lessons, activities, and instructional strategies throughout the year through an equity lens.

Let's Be Kind and Rewind.

Before we move on, let's summarize the proposed renovations to our Movie Theaters:

- **PLOT TWIST #1: Use Lecture Strategically.**
- **PLOT TWIST #2: Record Your Direct Instruction (If Possible).**
- **PLOT TWIST #3: Provide Support During Direct Instruction.**
- **PLOT TWIST #4: Set Time for Meaningful Processing & Retrieval.**
- **PLOT TWIST #5: Make it Interactive.**
- **PLOT TWIST #6: Promote Representation.**

Again, the key to making the most of our Movie Theater moments in our classrooms isn't to necessarily abandon this kind of teaching but to reflect on and renovate its weaknesses.

But what if we took an even deeper look into our classroom practices besides our Movie Theaters?

It's time for Blockbuster.

CHAPTER THREE

The Blockbuster Model

"Be kind, rewind."

The first Blockbuster store opened in Dallas in 1985. It's hard to put into words how truly revolutionary Blockbuster was. It offered something new. Instead of just going to the theater, anyone with a VCR/DVD player and a TV could choose from a vast selection of films. In just a few years, Blockbuster grew to over 9,000 US stores and into countries overseas. It commanded a vast inventory of titles. It employed tens of thousands of workers. It became a central part of Americans' desire for video entertainment. What really told you how popular Blockbuster was, though, were the contents of American wallets and purses in the 1990s. You could probably open most up and find at least three cards inside: a credit card, a driver's license, and a Blockbuster membership card.

Growing up, I always assumed that Blockbuster had, well, *always existed*, probably much the same as how kids today feel about Netflix or YouTube. I simply couldn't fathom how people had watched movies beforehand.

This is why Blockbuster serves as the perfect metaphor for how we've thought about teaching and learning in the past few decades. It feels like it's just how education *has always been*, at least recently. It's the use of textbooks as the basis of classroom learning, the repeated nights of busy work masquerading as homework, or the belief that students' access to learning is just limited to inside the classroom.

Just like the title of this book suggests, this model is in need of some serious breakage. But let's take a look at some of the then-transformational things that Blockbuster did do:

 The Blockbuster Experience

- Hundreds of titles were available across multiple genres.
- Movies could be watched by anyone with a TV and VCR/DVD player, and at a much lower price.
- Fast forwarding, rewinding, and pausing films let audiences watch at their own pace.

But for all of its innovations—including an innovative use of a barcode system to track rentals and late fees—we all know what happened as the years wore on. Blockbuster died at the hands of a new model of consuming content: Netflix. So what exactly was holding Blockbuster back?

Take 2   The Blockbuster Experience

- Movies could only be accessed by travel to a Blockbuster store.
- Late fees and other short-term rental policies caused frustration.
- Inventory was limited to what each store had on hand.
- Watching a movie was done at a whole-group, not individual, pace.

Of course, this isn't everything that ended Blockbuster as we knew it, but together, the positives and pitfalls of the store do provide a useful lens into classroom practices that we feel "have always been that way." So without further ado, here is the Blockbuster Model of teaching and learning:

The Blockbuster Experience

🎥 Content is centered on textbook use, and homework is given for its own sake.

🎥 Classroom rules are set and standardized.

🎥 Students' learning experiences are limited to what's physically available inside the classroom walls.

🎥 The pace of learning is variable, though it's modified for a whole group, not individual students.

So let's get to breaking it, shall we?

Plot 🔀 Point

PLOT POINT 1: If the Blockbuster Classroom Represents Obsolescence, Let's Deconstruct the Use of Textbooks.

In a lot of classrooms, saying "get out your textbook" is one of the quickest ways to get groans going (maybe only beaten by the occasional history-themed pun).

But let's be frank. Textbooks aren't well-liked. Teachers hate keeping track of them. Students hate carrying them.

And parents hate having to pay for them. So why do we still have them?

The use of textbooks dates back thousands of years and has sources in numerous cultures across the globe. It's the first wireless learning device, right? Though its purposes have shifted over time, the medium itself hasn't changed much. At its core, it's just words and pictures on paper.

Textbooks' longevity does have an upside. Like direct instruction, because they've been around for so long, there's a long paper trail (pun intended) of research on their efficacy.

Here's just a sample of what's been discovered:

- Students prefer hands-on learning compared to a textbook-centered curriculum (Foley and McPhee 2008).

- Whether using physical textbooks or newer digital textbooks, student achievement is generally the same (Daniel and Douglas 2013; Rockinson-Szapkiw et al. 2013).

- Representation (or the lack thereof) in textbooks, such as race, gender, and ethnicity, affects learning outcomes (Good, Woodzicka, and Wingfield 2010).

- Textbooks are expensive (no surprise here) and are getting more so. The average cost of textbooks for most college students is about $600 per year. From 2002 to 2014, they increased in price about three times the rate of inflation (Hill 2015).

But perhaps one of the most significant quotes I've read about textbooks comes from a piece by Dr. Yvonne Behnke (2018). She writes,

"Modern textbooks are called upon to go beyond the imparting of subject matter to students and to help teach competencies, skills, and 'powerful knowledge [...], such as key scientific concepts. The current state of affairs barely does justice to this lofty ambition [...]."

So if there's so much wrong with textbooks, why do we still use them? Or, if we *do* want to continue using them, could we repurpose them? Until we do, we're like Blockbuster: continuing to think that students will consume content the same way their peers did before them when times have clearly changed.

 NATE'S NOTE: *Don't know where to start with how to make the most of the textbook or ditch it outright? Check out Chapter 4: Spinoff Series: Getting the Most out of Blockbuster Moments.*

Plot ⮂ Point

PLOT POINT 2: We Don't Watch Movies Because We Need To. We Shouldn't Give Homework for the Same Reason, Either.

The debates over homework and its efficacy, appropriateness, and equity are vast and complex—too much for us to summarize in one book. But here's where our ongoing metaphor of Blockbuster can help us out by providing some outside perspective.

Take a moment and imagine that each evening, you were required to come home and watch a feature-length movie. Every. Single. Night. No skips.

You might be thinking, "Hey, that doesn't sound so bad. I like to watch Netflix often." There are a few other rules in this hypothetical:

- You have limited choice over what to watch.

- You're charged a fee of $5 each night you don't watch a movie.

- You may or may not have consistent access to a working TV or internet.

- Your worth as a person is judged by your ability to complete the task.

You probably see where this metaphor is going. **Homework is a mandatory Blockbuster membership our students didn't sign up for.**

Many of the problems with homework can be traced back to some underlying assumptions that have never seemed to go away. I call these "zombie" hunches about homework because, in the spirit of an undead horror flick, they just never seem to die.

"ZOMBIE" HUNCHES ABOUT HOMEWORK:

Homework teaches accountability.
There's actually no research to support that homework teaches responsibility or instills obedience (Kohn, 2006).

Students who do homework are inherently good. This is a dangerous assumption. To understand it, think about the inverse: because a given student lacks the supports necessary to complete work at home, does that make them inherently bad?

Lots of homework is a sign of rigor. Quality matters over quantity.

Students are motivated by behaviorism. Practices of rewards and punishments show up everywhere around homework, especially with grading. Research finds that many homework grading schemes cause what Goldberg (2007, 2012) refers to as a "homework trap":

Late work → points off → grades decline → attitude declines → avoidance of homework & resentment builds → more late work.

Adapted from Vatterott, Rethinking Homework: Best Practices That Support Diverse Needs, 2018.

It's pretty understandable why homework is so universally despised.

- Students hate it but know they have to complete it to get passing grades.

- Teachers feel like they have to give it, but they know that it might not be the right thing to do or are nervous about not giving it due to perceptions of "softness."

- Families see the stress it causes, but they want to make sure their students are doing the right thing.

- Forces outside the classroom believe homework is a way to promote responsibility and accountability, but research tells us it doesn't do that.

Where the debate over homework hits home for the theme of this book is the issue of UDL & equity. Dr. Cathy Vatterott, author of *Rethinking Homework* (2018), summarizes it like this:

DESPITE THERE being more diversity among learners in our schools than ever, many teachers continue to assign the same homework to all students in the class and continue to disproportionately fail students from lower-income households for not doing homework, in essence punishing them for lack of an adequate environment in which to do homework. At a time when demand for accountability has

reached a new high, research fails to prove
that homework is worth all that trouble.

Redesigning the practice of homework will be difficult, to be sure. But as teacher and author Matt Miller says, "the most dangerous kind of teaching is the one that doesn't take risks." And as it stands right now, rethinking our "cult(ure) of homework," to borrow a phrase from Dr. Vatterott, is simply too dangerous not to try. We'll show some specific techniques and research to back them up in the next chapter.

Just like we did for the Movie Theater Model, let's update our infographic before moving on:

The Blockbuster Experience

Content is centered only on textbook use and homework is given for its own sake. (But this doesn't reflect how students today best learn).

Plot ⮂ Point

PLOT POINT 3: Add Some Flexibility and Grace.

Just about every teacher in the United States and across the world in 2020 understood the need for those two words. COVID-19 strained educational systems, families, and students to the near-breaking point as we all scrambled to make the best out of extremely challenging circumstances. As teachers, our actions in the pandemic proved that we have an immense ability to improvise, adapt, and overcome.

Our efforts, though, could not hide the fact that COVID-19 exposed the long-standing issues and inequities in our educational systems, particularly in the United States. For all the cries for a "return to normal," I believe it's truly worth questioning if a complete reversal to "pre-pandemic teaching" is what we should want.

I often think about the things we regarded as super important before 2020: homework, dress code compliance, tardies, and late work, to name a few. Not to say those things don't matter to a degree, but when COVID hit, we shifted priorities toward what really mattered: our students, their learning, and the preservation of our collective sanity.

Grading late work, in particular, had always driven me up a wall as an educator. In my first year of teaching (2014-2015), I made the disastrous choice to penalize late work from students 15% each day an assignment was late. To no one's surprise, I quickly abandoned that strategy after a deluge of hard-to-compute grade calculations and lots of confusion from families and students. In the years after, I only accepted late work (for 50% off) if it was turned in before each unit's assessment. After that point, any work not turned in was a zero, a policy I stuck with until COVID arrived.

COVID forced me to take a big step back and reflect on my late work policies, but even more deeply, meditate on the values that my grades themselves prioritized. I had traditionally thought about my grades as a tug-of-war between three forces:

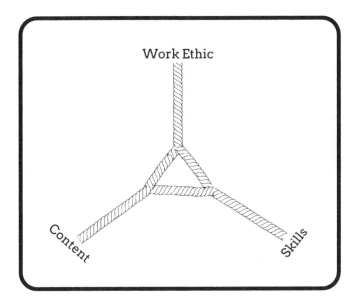

What I've come to realize, though, is that these forces of content, skills, and work ethic are much, much more complex than what appears. Each of these grading criteria, just like every practice in our classroom, carries hidden biases and assumptions (often referred to as the "hidden curriculum") that have profound effects on students' and families' perception of what is valued in our schools and classrooms.

My ropes, then (to continue the tug-of-war metaphor), became a little more frayed as I started to detangle and deconstruct my grading practices.

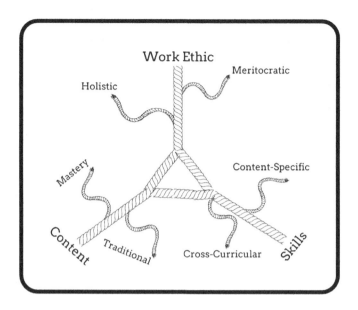

I love this infographic because it shows that our grading criteria are not only complex but often contain conflicting values.

- **CONTENT:** Do we believe mastery over time is more important than one's knowledge at a single moment?

- **SKILLS:** Which do we assess? Those skills only applicable to our own content or those that span across disciplines and into life?

- **WORK ETHIC:** Do our grading practices measure students equitably, or do they favor those with more privilege?

A lot of this introspection of grading practices can be painful. It was for me. A lot of the things *I believed* were important (in particular, late work policies, traditional assessments of content, and content-specific skills) had to be transitioned towards systems that were more student-centered, relevant, mastery-focused, and holistic.

Most scientific literature of the last few decades supports this shift away from traditional grading practices, especially ones that create situations where students can't dig themselves out. Researchers have known for a long time that grades can affect students' future performance, confidence, self-efficacy, and motivation (Brookhart 1994; Docan-Morgan 2012). But, as an article in the *Mid-Western Educational Researcher* notes:

> Traditional and still commonly used grading policies remain largely uninformed by accepted models of motivation, resulting in grading that often (and often unwittingly) produce opposite results from those intended (Covington, 1984; Kohn, 1993). Specifically under-considered in current grading schemes are the emotional effects that catastrophically low grades can have on student psyches. It is more than a simple truism that as much can be learned in failing as in succeeding. Research shows that students who sustain effort, even in failure, are more likely to see failure as temporary and as part of the learning process and will indeed learn from their mistakes when the failure is not crushing (Roediger & Finn, 2010). (Carifio and Carey 2013)

If this argument against strict behaviorism isn't hitting home, **picture the one thing that people hated about Blockbuster more than anything: late fees.**

Blockbuster collected some $800 million in late fees from its customers in 2000 alone. For me as a nine-year-old, I remember that having to pay late fees was the #1 reason my parents avoided going to Blockbuster, even more so if we knew that one of our movies was late anyway. There simply wasn't a chance, even partially, for redemption.

Let's apply this metaphor to students turning in late work. **If you know you've incurred $50 worth of late fees in homework, what would ever make you want to go back to class and have to pay for it?**

It's time for some more holistic approaches to our classroom practices that actually motivate students:

The Blockbuster Experience

🎥 Content is centered only on textbook use and homework is given for its own sake. (But this doesn't reflect how students today best learn).

🎥 Classroom rules are set and standardized. (Now let's add flexibility and grace).

NATE'S NOTE: *Truly Breaking the Blockbuster Model means that we also reconsider and revise other classroom practices besides grading. We'll explore more of these in the next chapter.*

Plot ⤷ Point

PLOT POINT 4: Extend Content Availability Beyond the Shelf.

Besides those late fees, perhaps nothing was worse about Blockbuster than this. You stride down the aisles, excited to find that movie you'd been thinking about renting, only to find that all of the copies are rented out! It's funny to think of what this would feel like today on a platform like Netflix or Amazon Prime. Imagine if they could only let 1,000 viewers watch a movie or show at a time! It just wouldn't work.

Very few of our students today take a "Blockbuster" approach to finding content. If they want to discover how something works, they check for a tutorial on YouTube. If they wonder what their friends are up to, they open Snapchat or Instagram. For them, a slew of online resources has replaced the limitations of what only their immediate physical surroundings can provide.

So, where's that Blockbuster shelf in our classrooms? It's that filing cabinet that was once the reliable go-to for activities, worksheets, or review packets. Or, it might be that aforementioned textbook that lurks under students' desks. Maybe it's the slide deck that can only be witnessed within your four walls, stored on a hard drive somewhere.

 NATE'S NOTE: *Although it might feel like we're heading to a digital-resources-only argument here, students shouldn't only work with material that's available online. Studies have consistently shown that students benefit from tactile, movement-based, and in-person learning. Some stuff simply can't be replicated in the cloud, nor should it be.*

Regardless of the shape they take, **Blockbustering content—making it only available in your classroom—can be a huge barrier to equitable access for your students and their families.**

But, when we ditch these barriers, we see positive effects:

- Families can support students outside of school.
- Students with particular needs can be better met, such as students with IEP's, 504's, English-Language Learners (ELL), and those with prolonged absences.
- Transparency of what teachers do opens up (which shows off the awesome stuff done in classrooms everyday).
- Teachers are positioned as a more accessible, accurate, and meaningful resource for students.

NATE'S NOTE: *Teachers benefit from this process too. Digitized resources mean we can better collaborate with colleagues in our own buildings and those across the world. I've taught in schools where I was on an island, and I credit the virtual connections I made at the time with preserving my sanity. Even though it was tough being alone, I was glad I had a digital boat to connect me to those beyond the horizon.*

In the next chapter, we'll highlight a way to "un-Blockbuster" your classroom with something called "cloning," as well as examine some tools to connect with other educators on a truly global level. For now, it's time for another infographic update.

The Blockbuster Experience

📽 Content is centered only on textbook use and homework is given for its own sake. (But this doesn't reflect how students today best learn).

📽 Classroom rules are set and standardized. (Now let's add flexibility and grace).

📽 Students' learning experiences are limited to what's physically available inside the classroom walls. (This barrier needs to be torn down).

Plot ⮂ Point

PLOT POINT 5: Blockbuster Gave Us Flexibility. Now, Let's Push Tailored Learning Experiences Further.

Blockbuster, in combination with VCR and DVD players, let us experience movies in a way not possible in theaters. Within the span of a rental of a few days,

Blockbuster let us pause, fast forward, rewind, and even watch an entire movie again as many times as we wanted.

In our classrooms, this practice of modification often appears as **differentiation,** which Dr. Carol Ann Tomlinson, a lead scholar on the topic, defines as:

"The idea of differentiating instruction is an approach to teaching that advocates active planning for and attention to student differences in classrooms, in the context of high-quality curriculums."(2009)

Differentiation is the bread and butter of good teaching. In short, it means that we meet our students where they are and make modifications to get them to where they need to be (that's Vygotsky's Zone of Proximal Development for you theory fans out there). Plus, the vast majority of teachers are excellent at it. We analyze, review, reinforce, tweak, elaborate, and reassess all the time.

 NATE'S NOTE: *How Can Teachers Differentiate?*

PROCESS: How students learn or interact with information.

PRODUCT: What students do/make to demonstrate their learning.

READINESS: Student's prior knowledge or skills.

PREFERENCE: What students choose to do.

CONTENT: What students learn.

ENVIRONMENT: The setup where students learn.

But differentiation does have its challenges. Many teachers (me included) are able to consistently differentiate through whole-group modification, but we struggle to find the time to personalize learning on that individual level that all students need.

 NATE'S NOTE: *A common myth about differentiation is that we only need to do it for students with IEPs, 504s, or other specific provisions in the classroom. Not at all! You'll find that differentiating for all students (giving those options of choice) really increases student buy-in and engagement.*

But notice how we've framed the issue so far: ***teachers have to differentiate for students***. And there's the problem: when we look at differentiation through just this lens, we have our limits. We're Blockbuster. We can easily vary the pace on *family* movie night, so to speak, but it takes a lot more time for us to get a single family member caught up on a missed episode.

So what's the solution? What most scholars have found is that individualized differentiation is possible, but not through even more teacher-led efforts. In fact, they found the opposite: **better differentiation means that teachers have to "let it go"** (insert a Disney musical here).

Let's break this idea down a little more. When I co-authored the book, *Don't Ditch That Tech* in 2019, we (my mom, Dr. Angie Ridgway, Matt Miller, & myself) studied the ideas of many theorists, such as Dr. Tomlinson and CAST's UDL framework. We even came up with our own model:

Teacher-Centric

Teacher-Led

Interactivity

Student-Chosen Process

Student-Chosen Content

**Student-Driven Content
& Quality Feedback**

Student-Centric

I'll summarize a major theme about differentiation we synthesized: **the more student-centric you want your classroom to be, the more control you have to relinquish.**

I can understand how this idea of letting go seems scary. When I've talked to educators, this fear is very common, as are a few others:

- "Creating alternatives, even if individual students are choosing from them, takes additional time."

- "Giving students more freedom in my classroom seems like an invitation for chaos."

- "How can I assess students doing so many different things at once? Nothing will be standardized."

I had these same worries, too, and they're very under-standable. I mean, imagine you've always used your neighborhood Blockbuster for movie rentals. Then, one of your friends down the street tells you, "Hey, there's this really new thing called Netflix where they send DVDs in the mail, and then you send them back when you're done." You have to admit; the idea would sound a little crazy if all you've ever known up until that point is your neighborhood video store.

All concerns aside, when more a personalized approach to differentiation can happen, researchers have found some pretty sweet benefits:

- It has a widespread, positive effect on students' learning experiences, from kindergarten to college (Hawkins 2009; Jacobse et al. 2019; Otaiba et al. 2011).

- Students are more intrinsically motivated, as well as more productive and creative (Amabile 1983; Bruner 1961; Jensen 1998; Sharan & Sharan 1992).

- Students allowed to explore areas of interest are more likely to do so in the future (Santangelo & Tomlinson 2009).

- Students tend to demonstrate their learning in ways that best fit their learning profile, which means a decision-making burden is lifted from teachers (Bailey and Williams-Black 2008).

- Students have a better perception of school and higher rates of achievement (Brighton et al. 2005).

In the next chapter, we'll explore some practical strategies to really break the Blockbuster Model. Before that, though, let's take the time to make a final edit to our infographic:

The Blockbuster Experience

- Content is centered only on textbook use and homework is given for its own sake. (But this doesn't reflect how students today best learn).
- Classroom rules are set and standardized. (Now let's add flexibility and grace).
- Students' learning experiences are limited to what's physically available inside the classroom walls. (This barrier needs to be torn down).
- The pace of learning is variable, though it's modified for a whole group, not individual students. (But now more than ever, students need learning that's tailored to their individual needs).

Let's get to the how of "Breaking Blockbuster," shall we?

CHAPTER FOUR

The Spinoff: Getting the Most from Blockbuster Moments

"WARNING! If this label is broken, you must purchase this video."

—BLOCKBUSTER **VHS**

In 2006, a group of scientists, tech professionals, educators, and industry leaders (from companies like Google and Microsoft) met at a workshop. Their job was a difficult one: conceive the textbook of the future. Would everything go digital and into the cloud? Would students still lug around books in backpacks? Or would it be something in-between?

After three days, the workshop wrapped up, and they shared their findings and recommendations. Instead of thinking about **form**, they answered the question of what the textbook of the future would look like in terms of **purpose**. This was their answer (as summarized by Bierman, Massey, and Manduca 2006):

"NO LONGER is information itself power; rather, power is gained from the ability to access the right information quickly."

So, the conference didn't deny a place for textbooks but implied that the format needed to be reenvisioned (at the very least) to better serve its users.

Similar to this workshop's findings, the Blockbuster Model that we encountered in the last chapter still has some elements that are worthy of use, but they're becoming archaic in their current state. Meeting the needs of today's students, especially in terms of access to resources, assessment practices, and differentiation, means change is a must. Our Blockbuster stores—educational systems, in this case—need to update before going out of business.

The challenge for us teachers is how to best tweak what we've got on hand—renovate our Blockbuster stores, if you will—without those changes becoming overwhelming to students, families, and ourselves. Let's check out some practical strategies to modify and maximize those Blockbuster Moments in our classrooms.

Plot ⤭ Twist

PLOT TWIST 1: Ditch (Most of) That Textbook.

Let's face it, at the end of the day, textbooks have two main strengths:

1. They're considered to be authoritative (though their credibility can sometimes be suspect due to bias).

2. They contain a lot of information.

In the last chapter, we explored some of the theoretical yet very real weaknesses of textbooks, such as engagement, representation, and equity. So what should we do? We'll let Matt Miller, author of the *Ditch That Textbook* series, give us some guidance.

Educator 📢 Voice

MATT MILLER
@jmattmiller

I quit my textbooks in 2007. I clearly remember my "burn the ships" moment when it happened. One day, I stood at my podium, asking my students questions from the end of the chapter of my textbook. I looked up at them. I saw disconnected students with this look on their faces: "I don't want to be here." I had seen this look a lot, and I couldn't take it any longer. Teaching straight from the textbook made learning feel pre-packaged and sterilized. So I had started deviating from the textbook, creating activities for my students based on their interests and personalities yet sticking to the curriculum.

I strayed more and more from teaching "by the book" until that fateful day in 2007. It dawned on me. If I quit my textbooks, I'll be forced to teach this way all the time. I mean, I'll *get* to teach this way all the time! I stopped in my tracks. Right in the middle of a lesson. I said, "Everyone, grab your textbooks." We locked them in my tall wooden cabinets in the corner of the classroom. Right in the middle of class. I never used them again.

I don't recommend quitting textbooks cold turkey for everyone. It was hard. I regretted my decision on days when I felt overworked, overwhelmed, and overtasked. Now that I'm on the other side of that decision, I've learned a few things about my decision to quit leaning on my textbooks:

Engagement can skyrocket. Textbook publishers don't know your students. When your classroom work looks and feels like them—even sounds like their jokes and guilty pleasures—students start looking forward to your class.

You have resources galore. The internet is packed with articles, videos, texts, audio recordings, primary sources, and so much more. It can be overwhelming at first, but when you find the treasure trove that matches your teaching, you'll never go back.

You can scaffold it just right. You know your students' abilities. By deviating from the textbook, you can suit your work for exactly what they need and differentiate accordingly.

The Textbooks of the Future
Resources

 Fluid: Resources can be updated quickly at no cost.

 Searchable: Subject matter is accessible and easy to navigate.

 Inquiry-Based: Information is structured more as a guidebook rather than an encyclopedia.

 Customizable: Information is tailored to each teacher's specifications. Other features might include use of local-centric information and scaffolded difficulty for individual students.

 Critical Thinking-Encouraged: While still providing a guidebook feel to information, the resource pushes students to make connections and meaning beyond what's obvious.

 Interactive: Students are encouraged to engage and "play" with their learning.

 Cooperative: Experts and novices alike can contribute to the resource collectively for the benefit of everyone.

Adapted from Bierman, P.; Massey, C.; and Manduca, C. (2006)

Strategy: Alternatives to Textbooks

As Matt mentioned, embarking upon a teaching voyage unanchored to textbooks can be scary. However, it can also be liberating. Imagine the possibilities of what a resource of the future could look like!

The research proposes that resources of the future should draw on these characteristics: **fluid, searchable, inquiry-based, customizable, critical thinking-encouraged, interactive, and cooperative.** (See graphic on previous page.)

So, where should we begin creating this tool of the future?

For one, **look for "organic intellectuals" around you—and those afar**. Very likely, you'll have naturally-developed resources created by fellow staff members or even colleagues much further away. In either case, rely on the strength of the internet—develop and share your own resources while remixing and improving upon the resources of others.

This leads me to another piece of advice: **develop a PLN** (professional learning network). A few years ago, educator Dr. Alec Couros shared a fantastic infographic on what a well-connected educator in a PLN looks like. Such an educator might utilize online communities, social networking services, videoconferencing, popular media, colleagues, blogs, and a range of other resources.

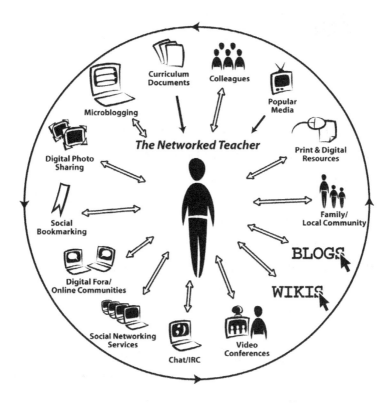

cc licensed (by-nc-sa); used with permission from Dr. Alec Couros

Notice the changes from just utilizing a physical textbook:

- There are near-unlimited sources of information in dialogue with one another.

- Information is connected to global sources.

- The teacher is now both a resource scavenger and producer who shares content and consumes it.

NATE'S NOTE: *If you'd like some more advice on how to get started creating a PLN, check out an e-book I authored here: tinyurl.com/edtechebook.*

How do you start? Take it slow. Developing a library of resources or a successful PLN doesn't happen overnight. It happens step by step, little by little.

Also, as you undertake the creation of your PLN, start thinking about how accessible your library of resources is—or could be. We'll explore this idea more later (read on!), but remember that quote from earlier: "No longer is information itself power; rather, power is gained from the ability to access the right information quickly."

Strategy: Textbook as Teacher Resource

One of my favorite ways to use a textbook in class is to use it for a single person. Me! If I'm trying to quickly jog my memory, get some clarifying information on a topic, or design a classroom activity, a textbook is a good place to start. Of course, I can have students use textbooks as a quick consult resource as well, but I prefer to have students learn from a source that's more interactive and meaningful than what a textbook can offer.

Strategy: Targeted Textbook Use

There's no requirement that *every* page of a textbook be used. Instead of assigning long readings, chapters, or even whole books en-masse, pull selections and snippets out that get the most bang for your buck. Odds are, there's a better and more meaningful way for students to engage with the rest of the material in another way. Here are the criteria I've used in the past to decide which parts of a text are worth including:

1. **"Does this source have an authoritative monopoly?"** Meaning, does the textbook have a perspective on a topic that cannot be found elsewhere?

2. **"Is the information inside the most meaningful or efficient way for them to learn that material?"** If not, turning to use another resource to accomplish that same task might be a better use of time.

3. **"Does this resource provide proper scaffolding for students?"** A text might be appropriate to use, but it may need additional scaffolding for students to be able to access it. Making modifications might be necessary before distributing it to students.

A recent lesson I used in my World Geography class shows an example of this kind of text. In one activity, I wanted students to practice working on literacy skills, specifically, summarization and interpretation of primary sources.

Before creating the resource you see below, I felt like I only was meeting one criterion from that previous list, specifically, that the text had really solid interpretations I felt like I couldn't find anywhere else.

However, I wasn't satisfied with the other two items on that list: the meaningful learning and the scaffolding. So, I decided to copy the text itself from the primary sources and used Google Slides to make a twist on the classic game *Street Fighter*, complete with visuals and sound bites from the game. Students loved the play on perspectives clashing and thoroughly enjoyed themselves. Doing the reading through Google Slides also made scaffolding easy; features like the dictionary and explore button were on hand to help students parse through tough parts.

Sometimes all it takes to make a source interesting is to give a snippet of it some flair and support.

James Marshall, judge of the Supreme Court of the Gold Coast Colony

An open letter in the newspaper, *The Gold Coast Leader*

It writes:

"The policy of indirect rule which this establishment was set up to pursue has some suspicious features about it and we have regarded it as our duty to put our people on their guard.... We think the best definition of indirect rule is, a system by which an alien government is enabled to place a Native State in the hollow of its hands and in such a way that it has only to pull the wires to start a Chief and his people dancing to its piping; it is a system by which the political officer can drive the wedge of divide-and-rule through any tendency on the part of the people to come together to develop political ideals.

Summarize the accusation the paper makes in your own words.
(type here) It says that...

Talk with your partner and debate and write:
Why is the word "improvement" a loaded term when used by the British?

He writes:

Whenever British rule is carried out and enforced according to European ideas, without consideration of the ideas equally ancient and equally deep rooted, which pervade the native mind, it may break and destroy, but without securing any real improvement.

My own experience of the West Coast of Africa is that that Government has for the time succeeded best with natives, which has treated them with consideration for their native laws, habits and customs, instead of ordering all these to be suppressed as nonsense, and insisting on the wondering negro at once submitting to the British Constitution, and adopting our ideas of life and civilization....

The natives of the Gold Coast and West Africa have a system of laws and customs which it would be better to guide, modify, and amend, rather than to destroy by ordinances and force. So they have their Chiefs and Court forms and etiquette, their own customs and mode of living which will not be improved by ridicule or forced abolition."

Summarize the argument he makes in favor of British indirect rule in a sentence:
(type here) He argues that...

Find a copy of the Google Slides reading here: bit.ly/38TjuAf

NATE'S NOTE: *Looking for ways to make digital text more accessible? Check out the tips and strategies found in Chapter 2!*

Plot ⤭ Twist

PLOT TWIST 2: Rethink Homework.

We've started renovating our Blockbuster stores—our classrooms. Now we can start modifying what students do with the videos that leave the shop: their homework.

We explored some of the mistaken assumptions about homework in the last chapter ("zombie hunches about homework"). Two examples: "homework teaches responsibility" and "the more homework given equates to rigor."

In this section, we get to take that theoretical exploration and make it pragmatic. **How can we change homework to better promote learning, access, and equity?** Let's explore some recommendations, strategies, and templates we can utilize in all grade levels and across subject areas.

Strategy: Quality Over Quantity

Research has long shown that student learning depends on a delicate balance between **meaningful thinking** and **repeated interaction** with material. What many students have experienced in the classroom, however, is more of the latter than the former. They get tons of practice, sometimes to the point that it becomes like busywork. However, they don't get much as much time to work with material in thoughtful ways.

My solution in my classroom has been to shift the homework paradigm away from "practice time" and toward "meaningful learning time." My students' work looks less like drills and worksheets and more like time to create and process.

Let's take something really basic—vocabulary—and see how we can switch from quantity to quality. In the spirit of my childhood, I'll give you this *totally self-invented* list of nonsense words for you to memorize:

NATE'S NOTE: *If you're not in on the joke here, memorizing these same words was a part of standardized tests in the early 2000s. Not even kidding.*

A "Blockbuster" approach to assigning vocab homework might have students look up the definition of the word, write its meaning, and then draw a picture. Not exactly the most engaging thing ever.

Instead, what if we took those same words and challenged students to make something much more interactive and meaningful, say, a vocab puzzle? And in just a couple of minutes, here's what we might create:

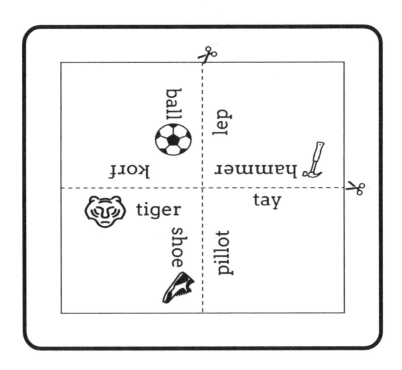

Once it's made, the pieces are cut out, and the puzzle is "solved" by rotating each piece until the borders match. Now, students have made something playable, turning a monotonous "drill and kill" exercise into something much more engaging.

NATE'S NOTE: *How can you tell if you're designing homework that has meaning? Ask yourself these two questions: Could this be a resource that students could use again to relearn? Does this assignment emphasize processing over repetition?*

Want to make some for your students or have students design their own vocab puzzles? Try this link:

bit.ly/vocabpuzzles

All that being said, don't think that homework with more meaning and less repetition is limited to humanities-related subjects like social studies and English. It's totally doable in math and science-related subjects, too! Stacey Roshan, a math teacher in Maryland, gives us some great advice on how to make homework more about the quality of thinking rather than the quantity of practice.

Educator 📢 Voice

STACEY ROSHAN
@buddyxo

There is no better way to learn than through teaching. We've all experienced this firsthand as teachers. The more we practice explaining, the deeper our understanding grows, and the better we are able to teach the material. How can homework give students the same opportunities to develop their understanding? Can they also gain deeper levels of empathy in their explanations of concepts by teaching their peers?

One activity that has been a game-changer in my math classroom has been video explanations of their math work. Here's why:

1. Awareness of students' own understanding

When recording video solutions, students are forced to talk the viewer through each and every step. In the process of recording, they become aware of any shaky spots or areas where verbalizing their thoughts is particularly challenging. This is a fantastic indicator, to both the student and the teacher, of areas that could use reinforcement.

2. Emphasis on process over product

In asking students to record a video solution to their problem instead of just "showing all work" on a piece of paper, I gain powerful insight into how students are thinking through their assigned problem. In grading these video solutions, I can easily put weight on the solution process over the final answer and reinforce to students that being able to effectively reason through a problem is more important than the final answer.

3. Celebration of multiple approaches

Students share not only their answer but their solution process. Then, they post those videos publicly for the class to view. This shows many unique approaches to solve a problem. A tool like Flipgrid extends this exercise. Students can comment directly under videos they've watched through typed text or a video reply. When they chat out their math thinking, students grasp complex concepts more deeply. Plus, they appreciate multiple perspectives for approaching the same problem.

4. Empathy in student-created content

I've built a library of student-created content over the years. I tend to use Flipgrid for student video creation. Those videos are always accessible through the Flipgrid topics I have created. Current students can add to topics that former students had responded to. We instantly build a library of video solutions created by students for students. This teaches empathy and awareness in a way we can't as teachers. Students understand what their peers are grappling with on an intimate level because they are in that struggle together. Powerful peer-to-peer learning can happen in this way.

5. Power of a global, authentic audience

Posting student videos publicly offers them an authentic audience, whether it's just our class or a more global audience. This audience promotes accountability and generosity, sharing with other students looking for help. This exercise requires students to go beyond simple computation. They must break down the concept as they would want it to be explained to them. With repeated practice, students become more adept at fluently describing the "why" behind their math logic. When motivation is low, this can be just the kickstart they need. Collaboration with peers from other schools is another powerful way to widen students' points of view. Flipgrid can be an ideal tool to help those students feel connected. It allows for two-way, asynchronous communication. Watching peers' videos and commenting on them can be a powerful metacognitive activity. Example: bit.ly/flipgridcollab

STACEY'S NOTE: *You'll notice that I use Flipgrid—a lot! What I love most about using Flipgrid in my math class, in general, is the ability to hear students talk through their solutions. This benefits the teacher and the student. It also helps the student self-identify what they do and don't know. So many times, students think their solutions are solid until they record. Then, they fumble to justify how to get from step a to step b. When I grade, that's really all I zone in on—student fluency, have they skimmed over certain key areas, etc.?*

Strategy: Equip Families to Support, Not Teach

All families want to see their students succeed. It's vital to equip them with a "support toolkit" for help. However, we need to tread carefully in terms of what's appropriate to expect from families. Research has pointed out that homework can marginalize and harm socio-economically disadvantaged students (Kohn 2006; Bennet and Kalish 2006; Kralovec and Buell 2000). The solution is to position families as a resource for student support, not a source of classroom-specific skills or content.

Here are three strategies I've used:

1. Communicate directly with families from the beginning of the year about homework. Solicit input from them. A partnership pushing for success is much stronger than a solo effort (Patton 1994; Shumow et al. 2011; Redding 2000; McNary et al. 2005). This is much, much easier today than it was even twenty years ago with the widespread use of apps like Remind, TalkingPoints, and other learning management systems.

2. Make sure that students and their families can complete homework without you or classroom resources present. Research shows that students struggle when assignments require extensive background knowledge or independent access to reference materials (Bennett-Conroy 2012).

3. Use the Flipgrid Camera to provide guidance and expectations on things sent home. I call this "Taking a Flipgrid 5." In less than five minutes, I can record a short explainer video, make some quick edits, and drop in a QR code that can be scanned & watched on any smartphone. In my own classroom, this has added some really powerful accessibility to my curriculum, whether I'm sending home a graphic organizer, a short reading, or a newsletter.

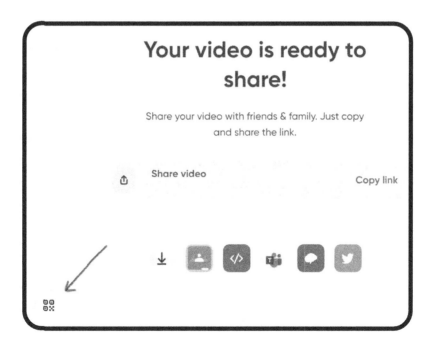

NATE'S NOTE: *Want to see Nate do this in action? Give these QR codes a try!*

Strategy: Tweak It!

Many other research-based modifications will have a positive effect on students' experiences with homework. For example:

- **Don't teach new material through homework.** In my own experience, this is a recipe for disaster, and outside scholarship confirms it, too (Cooper and Nye 1994; Patton 1994). There's a saying I've always followed since I became a teacher: *You can only teach one new thing at any given time: new content or new skills.* If you try to do both, you're going to struggle to figure out which your homework actually assesses.

- **Help students with self-regulation.** Think of these as the soft skills that make homework completion possible, such as setting goals, selecting appropriate learning strategies, maintaining motivation, monitoring progress, and evaluating outcomes (Bembenutty 2011). Develop self-regulation practices with students slowly and consistently over time.

- **Limit the amount of time that students spend on homework.** It's been found that in middle school, for instance, students who spend too much time on homework (more than 90 minutes) actually do worse than their peers who spend less time on it (Cooper et al. 2006; Shumow et al. 2011). Also, the grade-level and content-area team setups in many elementary and middle schools can help this. Teachers in these grades can space workloads out so that multiple tests, projects, and assignments don't hit like a sudden "homework tsunami."

App: Google Slides

Thousands of apps create more meaningful homework activities with countless more awesome ways to use them. To list them all here is impossible, like claiming, "I finished Netflix," or "I can explain *Tenet*." Because we can't list every app under the sun, let's check out one of my personal favorites:

NATE'S NOTE: *As we saw with Stacey's use of Flipgrid, it's important to always remember to* **start by considering the learning we want students to demonstrate first**, **then find an app that suits that learning best.** *This doesn't just apply to just homework. It's true with every moment in our classroom.*

www.streamlabs.com

Google Slides might be my favorite edtech tool ever created simply because of its flexibility and ease of use. As you might have seen from the examples in this chapter already, it's so much more than just a presentation tool. But it has a few other distinct advantages, such as being entirely based in the cloud (so no files are being passed back and forth), and up-to-the-second peer collaboration.

 NATE'S NOTE: *If you're a PowerPoint or Keynote user, no worries! You can adopt the same template ideas using Google Slides in those apps, too.*

Here's how I've used Google Slides to create meaningful homework assignments:

1. **Create Non-Editable Templates**

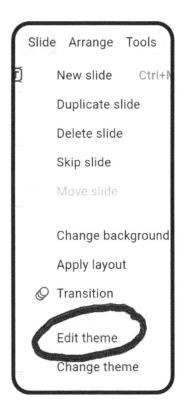

Using the "Edit Theme" option in the menu, create a background that students can't edit (perfect for graphic organizers, for example). Once finished, anything that students will need to interact with can be placed back on the slide itself. Remember, students just don't have to use text to respond. Interactive elements can include audio with Mote (www.mote.com), icons from Flat Icon (flaticon.com), or royalty-free pictures from Unsplash (www.unsplash.com). Note: all of these integrate into Google Slides and are student-friendly.

Here's an example of what Sundown town (and efforts to make one) would sometimes look like.

Make sure to read the caption, too.

Highlighter

(Special to the News.)

HUNTINGTON, Ind., Jan. 9.—A petition signed by 328 persons, asking that Huntington's negro population be deported was filed with Mayor Charles cGrew late "Wednesday. The petition sets forth that the negroes were imported for war work in a foundry, and charges that the conduct of the colored men, of whom there are only eight, has not been of the right sort and may start a race riot. The petition also says that the negroes have been given preference in labor at the foundry, to the exclusion of white men who have been long- time residents of Huntington.-. Huntington has never had more than two negro families at any one time until after the United States entered the war, when several negro moulders were imported. Before that time negro transients' were given warnings to move on and spread the word that they were not welcome in the city. The labor trouble is said to be primarily responsible for the petition, as threats have been made against the colored folks.

A story from the Fort Wayne News-Sentinel from January of 1919 talks about a petition filed with the mayor of Huntington to have the Black residents be ordered out of town. The article also states that, before the first World War, the town had never had more than two Black families because they would be run from town. (CLICK TO ENLARGE.)
Credit FORT WAYNE NEWS-SENTINEL

Finally: Leave a Mote:

1. For your final response, leave a voice recording using Mote.

2. Following the directions using the GIF →

3. When finished, drag your voice recording here:

Finally: Leave a Mote:

Summarize 3 things you learned about the urbanization of Indianapolis and make 2 connections of the city's history to today.

bit.ly/indyurbanize

Want to create your own interactive Google Slides assignments? Watch a tutorial on how to do this here: bit.ly/ slideswalkthrough

Nate R

Making simple changes to Google's Share URLs can really change how you distribute documents and other files. Here are just a couple of examples. (Caution: Be sure you've made the file available to students with the Share button first!)

Force-Copy: Make students automatically create a copy of the document shared with them. This is particularly useful for template sharing.

- How to Do It: Change the word "edit" in the share URL to the word "copy."

Auto-Present: Make a student automatically enter presentation mode in a Google Slides file. This means that they can't see the thumbnails of other slides in the presentation sidebar. This can be useful for Choose Your Own Adventure-style games, virtual museums, hiding slide notes, or holding back content for a dramatic reveal.

- How to Do It: Change the word "edit" in the share URL to the word "present."

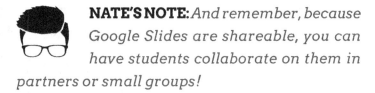

NATE'S NOTE: *And remember, because Google Slides are shareable, you can have students collaborate on them in partners or small groups!*

2. Create kinesthetic activities

Remember that vocab puzzle activity earlier in this chapter? Google Slides can be used to create digital versions of kinesthetic activities like that. It's perfect for practicing meaningful learning in the classroom or at home. Using the Non-Editable Template and "Force Copy" tricks mentioned before, have students sort traits onto t-charts, design Venn-diagrams, or even play board games to process their learning. Here are three examples from my own classroom you can try:

T-Chart Sorting

Sort the different forces onto the appropriate side. There might be answers that apply to both. Check your answer using the key on the next slide.

Centrifugal Forces	*Centripetal Forces*

Ethnic Unity
Social Injustice
Nationalism
Ethnic conflict
Poverty
Social Equity
Just / Fair Legal System
Charismatic Leadership
Religious Acceptance
Common Heritage
Religious Intolerance
Common Language
Dictatorial Leadership
Loss of Rights

Venn Diagram

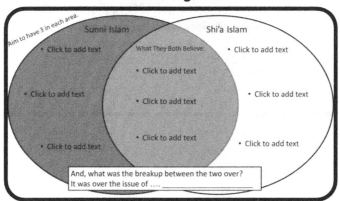

Board Games

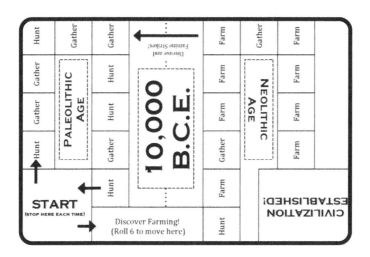

T-Chart Sorting	Venn Diagram	Board Game
Link: bit.ly/slidestchart	Link: bit.ly/slidesvdiagram	Link: bit.ly/slidesboardgame

Plot ⤭ Twist

PLOT TWIST 3: Rethink with Flexibility & Grace in Mind.

Last chapter, we took a hard look at the need for more flexibility and grace in a post-COVID world, especially in regard to grading practices.

With that in mind, where do we begin? David Frangiosa, a fellow educator, offers this advice: **Think about what your grades say.**

Educator 📢 Voice

DAVID FRANGIOSA
@DavidFrangiosa

Oftentimes, we use the terms "assessment" and "grading" interchangeably. While they are related, they are not the same thing.

I wanted to understand the purpose of my assessment and grading practices. What information was I trying to collect? What did I want to communicate to students? As I started pulling at that thread, what I found was that my grades were not reflective of my values.

What I value as an educator has been consistent since the beginning of my career. I have always wanted students to learn for the sake of learning, acquire skills and knowledge, and apply those understandings to new situations. I soon realized that the message I was sending with traditional grading was contradictory to the values I was expressing to students.

The acquisition of knowledge and development of skills is a process. An imperfect, messy process. In a traditional model, all of that messy practice was scored and cemented forever in a grade book. This caused students to strive for perfection instead of growth, which contradicts everything I believe in. Every effort I made to provide constructive feedback was undermined by the pursuit of a "good grade." Conversations fell flat. The time I took to mark papers? Wasted. The students were in survival mode. In their mind, they had to figure out how to navigate my class with the least damage done to their GPA. It wasn't enjoyable or productive for anyone and needed to change.

I have come to view assessment as a process of determining where a student is in their learning journey. Part of assessment is the process of identifying the tools and support necessary for students to progress. Information collected from assessment can be summarized in grade form, but the grade is not necessary for learning to occur. In fact, the presence of a grade can inhibit the process. The goal is to shift student focus away from grades and back to learning. This requires a mindset shift by both teacher and student.

> Regardless of intention or approach, your message can be undermined by the presence of a grade. How many times during a conversation have you had students ignore your suggestions to ask, "what do I need to do to get an A?" The pressure they are under to perform and achieve is tremendous. I don't blame them for trying to play the game of school and get their grade. However, when that mentality enters the learning process and becomes the focus, it can inhibit learning.

 NATE'S NOTE: *If you'd like to learn more about how David went gradeless, check out this resource: bit.ly/gogradeless*

You'll notice that David talked much less about the "how" of grades: percentages and specific standards; and much more about the "why" behind them. With that in mind, what are some "hows" that can help us shift toward extending flexibility and grace in our classrooms?

Our parents always told us to avoid R-rated movies (you know, with adult content not suitable for those under 17 years old). Instead, here are three R's that can help us rethink our classroom practices. Each "R" represents a step towards making this transformation happen.

R	**REFLECT**
	IS WHAT I'M DOING WORKING?

1. **Reflect.** When we reflect or ask, "Is what I'm doing working?" we're evaluating current practices to see if they really do help families, students, communities, and us teachers accomplish our goals. We might take a hard look at policies such as giving detentions for tardies to class. Do they actually change behavior for students that are consistently late? Or, we might take a hard look at our late work policies. What effects do they actually have on work completion?

R	**REORIENT**
	WHAT DO I VALUE?

2. **Reorient.** The question, "What do we value?" gets to the heart of what we want as educators from our students and our classrooms. Obviously, I can't answer this for you, but ideally, our values should reflect our practices and vice-versa. If they don't, one of the two needs to change.

R	**RELATIONSHIPS**
	FAMILIES - STUDENTS -
	TEACHERS - SCHOOL

3. **Relationships.** Relationships are the sin-gle-most-important factor in the classroom. They're the key to everything. Period.

When we extend flexibility and grace, we're really refocusing classroom behaviors away from following policies and towards cultivating relationships.

Relationships—actually, the lack of them—is why Blockbuster's late fee system never worked. Turning in a movie late to Blockbuster (you younger teachers, just imagine it, if you can) meant you paid the fee, felt annoyed, and ultimately moved on. And truthfully, Blockbuster didn't want a relationship with us. Blockbuster actually didn't want us to be better with our returns. Profit was the goal. (Remember that our practices should match our values?)

But let's re-imagine the scenario. Instead of Blockbuster, picture yourself in the early 2000s (with highlights in your hair, low-waisted jeans, and NSYNC on the radio, of course) visiting a local mom-and-pop video store. Your neighbor, who you've known for years, owns it. And this time, when you walk in, you return one of your rentals late, but because there's a long-standing relationship, you promise to have the next one back on time. And because you care, you do.

And that's the difference: **relationships, with flexibility and grace in mind, have the power to create meaningful change.**

Plot ⤭ Twist

PLOT TWIST 4: Tailor the Student Experience

For all of Blockbuster's failures, there was one thing it did better than any other store at the time: give families options for what they wanted to watch. They even curated local stores' selections based on what was locally popular! In the teaching world, this is what we call "differentiation," and last chapter, we noted these points about it:

1. Differentiation is at the core of quality teaching.

2. It's easier to differentiate for groups of students than for individuals.

3. More intensive, individualized differentiation actually requires that we *let go* of control.

4. A differentiated classroom results in a more student-centric experience. This has a bunch of benefits for teachers and students alike, ranging from productivity to perceptions of school.

Differentiation moves learning away from a "one-size fits all" approach and tailors students' experiences to individually meet their particular needs.

 NATE'S NOTE: *Don't forget! In Chapter 1, we discussed the framework of UDL (Universal Design for Learning). Remember, it's centered on the philosophy of accessibility, especially with how students engage, process, and express their learning. UDL has a large role to play, too—as you'll see—in tailoring students' experiences in the classroom.*

But here's where I'm going to leave you on a bit of a cliff-hanger. We may already do a great job of differentiating like Blockbuster (whole-group, with a few options to choose from). Are you ready to take the next step on our metaphor?

It's time to "See What's Next": the Streaming Model.

Let's Be Kind and Rewind.

The proposed renovations to our Blockbuster stores are to:

- **PLOT TWIST #1: Ditch (Most of) that Textbook.**
- **PLOT TWIST #2: Rethink Homework.**
- **PLOT TWIST #3: Rethink with Flexibility & Grace in Mind.**
- **PLOT TWIST #4: Tailor the Student Experience.**

CHAPTER FIVE

The Streaming Model

"See What's Next."
—Netflix

Let's face it: there was a lot going on around the turn of the millennium. MP3 players replaced Sony Walkmans and were filled up with albums from NSYNC, Eminem, Jay Z, and the occasional Nickelback song. (Mistakes were made with that last one). Cell phones could no longer serve as handy doorstops; some even flipped open. The word *blackberry* no longer referred to a fruit. And most importantly, for this book, movie watchers turned to a new invention called DVDs as an alternative to VHS tapes.

It's easy to forget (kids today certainly do) that Netflix began with DVDs. But over time, things changed. According to one study, Americans now do 26% of their TV-watching as streaming, and the number is growing (Neilsen 2021). My own family currently has subscriptions to several such services. You probably do as well.

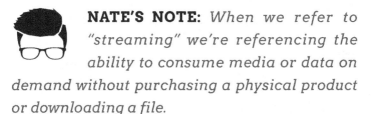

NATE'S NOTE: *When we refer to "streaming" we're referencing the ability to consume media or data on demand without purchasing a physical product or downloading a file.*

Streaming has transformed the digital landscape of television and movies. Newer mediums such as YouTube, Twitch, and TikTok continue to push the boundaries of content sharing. But why did streaming become a thing? What makes it so much better than going to Blockbuster? Truthfully, it's hard to say where the advantages start, but if I had to rank my top three, I would choose:

1. No more traveling to a physical store or having to manage DVD cases.

2. No more late fees.

3. Much, much more content is available.

For the purposes of this book, we'll summarize streaming like so:

The Streaming Experience

🎥 Content is available anywhere, anytime.

🎥 Material is personalized for viewers, makes connections, and impacts beyond the content itself.

🎥 Streaming services are constantly updated, adaptable, and focused on improvement.

As you might have guessed, **The Streaming Model is the next step in our metaphorical exploration of learning design**. So what exactly is it? The Streaming Model shifts our classrooms away from the teacher-centric feel of the Movie Theater Model. It deviates from the traditional takes on teaching in the Blockbuster Model. Instead, we craft an entirely new experience centered upon *access, equity, relevance, and reflection.*

The Streaming Experience

🎥 Classrooms have a digital clone that can be accessed anywhere, anytime.

🎥 Content is individualized and relevant, and underlying, cross-curricular skills are emphasized.

🎥 Instruction is dynamic, flexible, and focused on growth over time.

Let's break it down. (Note: You may have noticed that in Chapters 1 and 3, I offered plots: the way things are. Then, in the following chapters, Chapters 2 and 4, you got the plot twists: the way things could be. In this chapter, I'll give you the plot and then the plot twist to offer solutions immediately.)

Plot ⤳ Point

PLOT POINT: Break The Blockbuster Model

Yep, it's finally time to talk about this book's namesake. It's time to "Break the Blockbuster Model." We need to rethink and/or move beyond teaching and learning the way they've always been. To borrow a phrase from a Netflix ad, it's time to "See What's Next."

"But what about that idea of getting back to normal? Isn't that what we should want?"

It's a well-intended thought. Pandemic fatigue is real, especially for educators, families, and administrators. **However, I think it's worth questioning if that "normal" we're desperate for, unchanged and unaltered, is worth returning to.**

COVID-19 continues to (as of this writing) highlight and exacerbate long-standing inequities and barriers in pre-K to collegiate education. When the pandemic hit my home state of Indiana in March of 2020, it was obvious that schools and students with *more access and privilege* (think Chromebooks, wifi, childcare, etc.) could shift to digital learning with greater ease, while those with *less access and privilege* were left scrambling. As the US Department of Education acknowledges, impacts from COVID fell "disproportionately on students who went into the pandemic with the greatest educational needs and fewest opportunities—many of them from historically marginalized and underserved groups" (2020).

You might have noticed some of these inequities underscored by COVID in schools near you, maybe even in your own classroom. It might have been a student with an IEP (individualized education plan) who struggled or a close colleague who felt burned out or overwhelmed from lack of support. COVID should give us all the fuel we need to carefully reconsider and redesign a "new normal."

Change works best from the bottom up. As teachers and school leaders, we can break the Blockbusters in our classrooms and communities to promote equitable access to learning.

Let's see how.

Plot ⤨ Twist

PLOT TWIST 1: Clone Your Classroom

What's a teacher's most valuable resource? Coffee? A free T.A.? A new computer and a strong wifi signal?

I'd argue it's time. There's so much we have to do as teachers. Grading. Going over standards. Learning about blood-borne pathogens. (Do you have to watch that gory training video at back-to-school time, too?) They seem to get in the way of what brings us joy: helping students.

One of the first solutions to my dwindling time resources was flipped instruction. I liked the potential it had to make my class more efficient and improve student learning. Flipped instruction is where students work on direct instruction activities at home, like watching recorded lectures or completing readings. In-class time is spent on active practice and collaborative learning.

I started flipping my classroom in 2015. I started researching flipped classroom models, and I had conflicted feelings about it. What bothered me the most was the definition: "Direct instruction at home, practice at school."

Fundamentally, flipping didn't solve my Blockbuster classroom's brick and mortar problems. It just digitized them. Whether digital or paper, traditional or flipped, ineffective teaching practices are still ineffective teaching practices.

There had to be a better answer.

Then, it hit me: **Why flip *just* direct instruction? What would it look like if I flipped *everything*?**

This idea became what I now call "cloning," creating a digital copy of my classroom that mirrors—to the greatest extent possible—my physical one and is accessible to students, their families, and myself, 24/7/365. Take a look at this small example!

tinyurl.com/clonedclassroom

Cloning is what turned streaming services like Netflix, Hulu, and Amazon Prime into a common part of people's lives. Want to watch *The Great British Baking Show* on your Alexa Echo Show while cooking? Yup. Looking to stream *Succession* on your smart TV? Easy. Need to catch that latest episode of *The Mandalorian* on your smartphone while working out? Done. The point is this: **viewers stay engaged if streaming services meet them where they are. Why shouldn't our classrooms do this, too?**

For the record, cloning isn't the same thing as digitizing or just uploading content onto an LMS. Cloning also thinks about the underlying skills, thinking, and collaboration that traditionally happen in person and tries to make them more accessible, too.

 NATE'S NOTE: *Yes, cloning **is** a more tech-infused method of lesson design, but just remember:*

1. *Not everything has to be cloned, nor can or should it be.*
2. *The point of cloning isn't to add to our plate. It should ultimately give us more time to focus on what matters: our students.*
3. *Not everything has to be cloned at once.*

Is cloning worth the time? **Yes.** It pays for itself by the first time a student asks, "What'd I miss last class?" When COVID hit my school, 60% of my students were absent due to positive tests, quarantines, or having to provide childcare for younger family members. Meeting these students' needs was, in a word, challenging. However, **cloning gave my students the best chance I could for them and their families to have equitable access to learning.**

The advantages of a cloned classroom are immense! Here's a summary, with a nod to all the *Star Wars* fans:

How Cloning Helps Our Padawans:

 Allows students more flexibility to learn in terms of time (ahead of schedule, behind schedule, as review, visual for language support, etc.).

 Equips students' families with the same content and skill knowledge, allowing them to become more involved in their child's day-to-day schooling.

 Positions teachers as more positive, accurate, and meaningful resources for students.

Better meets the needs of students who need additional exposure to skills and content, such as students who:
- ★ Have IEP's (Individualized Education Plans)
- ★ Are ELL's (English Language Learners)
- ★ Are students with extenuating circumstances such as prolonged absences, moving to/from another school, etc.

NATE'S NOTE: *The Cloned Classroom is based on an extension of the ideas found in UDL, which we briefly met back in Chapter 1. At its core, we're creating what CAST (the creators of the UDL framework) refer to as "providing multiple means of action and expression" (2018). We're breaking down the barriers that hinder students' access to learning, and doing so with equity in mind.*

Want to see how it looks in a classroom? Benjamin Cogswell, a kindergarten teacher in Salinas, California, shares his cloning experience below.

Educator Voice

BENJAMIN COGSWELL

@cogswell_ben

One day, I was teaching a few lessons on addition with number bonds—a graphic organizer to teach addition with two parts and a whole. I noticed some students just weren't getting it.

I don't know why, but I decided to take out my smartphone, gave it to one of my kindergartners, and I asked them to record a video of me. After the lesson was done, I used my phone to quickly upload my recently filmed, and probably imperfect, lesson for student consumption. Then, I sent students back to their seats, had them open up their Chromebooks, and told the students to watch the lesson on their devices as many times as they felt they needed to and complete the activity.

What happened next amazed me. As I walked around, I noticed some students were more engaged in the lesson on the screen than the lesson seated on the carpet. Some students watched the lesson a few times before starting. Others started immediately on their additional tasks without watching the video at all. Even more awesome: a few families watched my video at home.

I realized that I could be available to my students at a time that worked best for them. The whole process didn't take extra time or preparation. It just took a smartphone.

As time went by, the creativity and content in my lessons soared. I realized that I could tie an instructional video to each lesson in my learning management system, Seesaw. Here are a few examples of cloned videos or activities I've made in the past that you can try yourself!

- Going on a Letter Hunt: bit.ly/goingletterhunt
- Finger Counting From 1 to 10: bit.ly/countingonetoten
- Looking for more tips & tricks with Seesaw? Check out my YouTube channel: bit.ly/BenCogswell

Once complete, these resources can be used by students at any time, in any place, and as many times as they would like. I still use these videos with students face to face in class. Often, I'll now teach the lesson first and provide the video as a supplement to my lesson or a reteach or review.

You might decide to go all out and create your own material. You might just use someone else's you find online. Regardless, cloning your classroom gives students choice and access to content that is always available, rewindable, and replayable. All it really takes to get started is a smartphone or a screencast application and, of course, you, the teacher.

So, ready to give cloning a try? Here's how:

How To Clone Your Classroom:

1. Break It Down

Deconstruct your standards, content, and other skills you need to teach, just like normal.

2. Create/Curate

Build/collect your lesson materials. Start thinking about how students and families can access these materials.

3. Support

Take a step back and think about scaffolds. Create any underlying supports might users need if they use the digital clone independently.

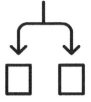

4. Distribute

Publish your lesson and use your cloned setup in class. Students and families can access what they need before, during, or after class.

You might have noticed that cloning your classroom is not really that different from what you already do in the classroom—and that's the point! Cloning only changes *how students and their families access and interact* with what we already do in the classroom. Think of it like an amplifier on a speaker. It makes your awesome teaching felt more equitably across—and beyond—your classroom.

One last quick note about cloning. It does have its limitations.

- Some materials can't or shouldn't be cloned, like whole-class simulations or classroom community building exercises. Tech can only do so much.

- Cloning does involve a varying level of up-front time investment, but it will pay off in the future. Think of it like Marvel working on their next super-hero film. The studio has to film first before they can rake in the box office revenue.

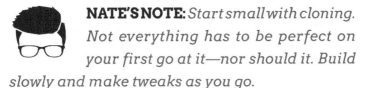 **NATE'S NOTE:** *Start small with cloning. Not everything has to be perfect on your first go at it—nor should it. Build slowly and make tweaks as you go.*

Suggestions for Cloning

These are some of my own favorite apps that make cloning possible, but you might have tools of your own that better fit your preferences and/or your students' needs. Think of this area as a "recommended watchlist" if you're looking for new and better tools.

NATE'S NOTE: *The rule "quality over quantity" really applies with cloning, but really with edtech in the classroom in general. A token number of apps can empower students (and faculty, too!), but having to navigate dozens of them gets in the way of success. Develop a small toolkit with accessible, reliable, and effective digital tools for your purposes.*

App: Your Learning Management System

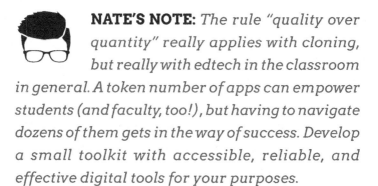

No surprise here. LMSs (learning management systems) can efficiently and quickly distribute cloned content. In many cases, your school likely requires an LMS like Canvas, Brightspace, Seesaw, or Google Classroom. If it doesn't, or you don't have an LMS yet, no worries. More on that in a second.

NATE'S NOTE: *It's key to understand that just using an LMS isn't the same as cloning with an LMS. Watching a trailer for an upcoming film isn't the same as experiencing the whole movie, right? Cloning emphasizes a parallel physical and digital experience.*

Using your LMS to clone your class isn't that complicated. You might be doing lots of solid cloning practices already.

Strategy: Consider Accessibility

Consider and test how students, not just you, access your content. Here are some key questions I ask myself when creating:

- **Is my clone friendly to students with inconsistent or slow internet?** There are a few ways to address this. One option: limit the amount of data transfer involved in your assignment. This includes large file downloads, video streaming, and video conferencing. If students need to download something, downloading it at school before going home is ideal. Make file sizes small if they must access them from home.

- **Can my lesson be easily viewed and completed using a variety of devices?** Can students do their work on an iPad, a smartphone, or a laptop? This is especially important if you're at a BYOD (bring your own device) school.

- **Are passcodes or subscriptions required?** If yes, just remember that each typed-out login is a potential barrier. Giving students a link to click that logs into an app automatically is better than typing multiple letters and numbers.

- **Are my materials available in multiple languages?** This isn't always possible or easy to do, even if you have the time, but certain apps can help. Immersive Reader (a Microsoft app built into Edge, Pear Deck, Flipgrid, and others) and Google Docs offer translation. To clone in multiple languages, I have generally found apps that can do it for me. If not, I'll approach particular needs on a case-by-case basis.

Providing student support (aka scaffolding) is important, especially with edtech and apps in mind. It can vary widely depending on student needs and your own preferences. I've already mentioned Pear Deck, Immersive Reader, & Insert Learning as examples. I'd be remiss not to mention this one:

App: iorad

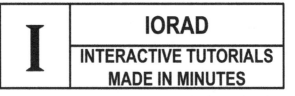

Iorad constructs digital, interactive tutorials for whole lessons, station work, teacher sick days, or even families at home. These walkthroughs look like a simple collection of screenshots, but they're much more. By recording your clicks, iorad builds a virtual experience where users get to practice the actions they'll need to perform later. Iorad also features automatic translation into hundreds of languages and text-to-speech generation. Tutorials only take about 5 minutes to make and are shareable/embeddable in just about anything. Find it here: www.iorad.com and give a tutorial a try here: ior.ad/7EQx.

> **NATE'S NOTE:** *Remember, cloning shouldn't be exclusively digital. Providing paper copies to students is something I always do. Many students will prefer using paper to other digital alternatives.*

Strategy: Streamline

Think about organizing your content in the way your favorite streaming platform does. Most platforms have a few things in common: some kind of login/landing page, a selection page, and, finally, a viewing/watching page. Even if you don't follow this setup (everyone has their preference), strive for fewer than five clicks for student's to find what they need. Every click a user has to make is a barrier. If it takes ten clicks to get to where you need to go, cut steps out.

NATE'S NOTE: *Log on to Netflix, Hulu, or Amazon Prime and give the five-click rule a try. Seriously! Did it work? There's a reason designers think this way; it's more accessible!)*

Strategy: Create Order

Organize your content around a central landing page and some kind of ordering mechanism, such as units, dates, etc. Streaming platforms do this, too. They'll use themes, genres, or mediums, like TV shows or movies. It helps users find what they need. Take a look at my order in my Google Classroom.

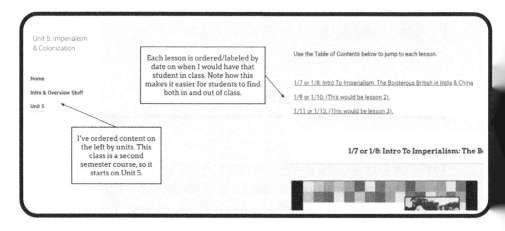

There's no one right way to organize content in your LMS, but it should always feel intuitive and mirror how you present your lessons in person. Because my high school students are on a block schedule, I put my material on Google Classroom into units and specific dates rather than have Friday/Monday lessons be split across different weeks, for instance.

Strategy: Build an LMS

Don't have a learning management system? No worries. Some LMSs, like Canvas and Google Classroom, let individual teachers sign up for free independent of their school districts. However, there are even simpler solutions than that.

Building a simple LMS doesn't take long and doesn't cost anything. You can use HyperDocs, a student-centered, pedagogically sound, digital lesson design format. HyperDocs were created by California educators Lisa Highfill, Kelly Hilton, and Sarah Landis; you can find more information at hyperdocs.co.

Below are two examples. My mom, Dr. Angie Ridgway, a college professor, created the first inside a Google Doc. I made the second inside Google Slides. Feel free to steal these examples as templates to create your own! Also, you can check out this guide for more on how to get started with HyperDocs: bit.ly/flippedebook

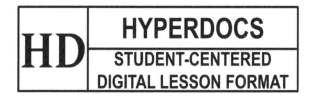

NATE'S NOTE: *You can always create HyperDocs to use inside of an LMS, too!*

Ready to share student work in documents like these? Follow a few key guidelines:

1. Share the day's lesson and objectives.

2. Provide links to the day's content, activities, and assessments.

3. Provide a common place where students can turn in work.

4. Be organized and look engaging.

NATE'S NOTE: *One of my teacher friends in Indiana, Nadine Gilkison (@nadinegilkison), has a fantastic collection of free HyperDocs you can check out here: bit.ly/nadinehyperdocs.*

Plot ⤨ Twist

PLOT TWIST 2: Differentiate Like the Algorithms Do

Blockbuster tried to tailor its movie selections to local communities' tastes. Streaming took that idea even further with algorithms that personalize selections on an individual level. Nowadays, Amazon Prime features "Movies We'll Think You'll Like," Netflix offers "Top Picks for(insert your name here)," and Hulu has a "For You" collection.

Why do streaming services go to all the trouble of personalizing recommendations?

The answer: **Interest and choice drive engagement.** Because streaming algorithms tailor our viewing and give us options, we often spend more time watching than intended: "binging," right?

There's a lot we can take away from the metaphor. We know that:

- Students thrive when they can see themselves in their classrooms.

- Student "buy-in"' increases when they're offered choices that empower them.

What streaming services do, essentially, is *differentiate the viewing experience for each user.* The Streaming Model attempts to do the same thing, but with learning.

 NATE'S NOTE: *For more evidence on how differentiation contributes to positive effects on student learning, see Chapter 3.*

Anyone suggesting we need to individualize learning through the Streaming Model, though, has to recognize the difficult moment that many educators are in right now. As a profession, we're overextended, overstressed, and overburdened with everything from continued fallout from

COVID to outside political pressure. The last thing many educators need is another thing added to their plates.

That's why the Streaming Model, ideally, centers differentiation on teachers "letting go" and puts students at the heart of decision-making, especially around those practices found in our Movie Theaters & Blockbusters. And, make no mistake, this is a win-win for both parties. Teachers get to save some sanity, and students feel heard.

There've been many, many books written about how to differentiate on a more personal level, but for our purposes, we'll focus on three practical strategies to get started. They aim to balance meeting students' needs while avoiding putting undue burden on us.

> **NATE'S NOTE:** *For more edtech specific ways to differentiate, check out* Don't Ditch That Tech: Differentiation in a Digital World, *by Dr. Angelia Ridgway, Matt Miller, and myself!*

Strategy: Slow-Drip Differentiation

A big misconception about teaching, especially for newer teachers, is that everything has to be perfect right away, especially when giving students options and choices. This felt especially true for me in my teacher prep program (which my mom was actually in charge of). In order to graduate, we had to craft three highly-differentiated lessons for our end-of-semester portfolios. While the experience taught me a lot, differentiation on an everyday basis simply can't work like that—and neither should most lessons, at least at first. Feedback from students, assessments, and other sources should inform our differentiation on a day-to-day basis. (Love you, Mom!)

A much more reasonable approach is ***slow-drip differentiation.*** This means adding choices over longer stretches of time. Think of it like streaming your favorite TV show: they don't drop all ten seasons at once. Neither should we! I slow-drip differentiation throughout the year in my classroom through process, content, and demonstration of learning.

Slow-Drip Differentiation Examples

Process

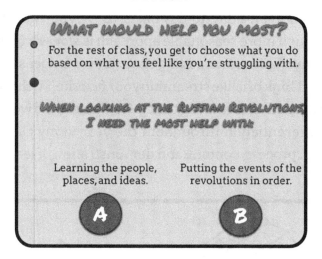

After teaching the history of the Russian Revolution the first time and having students make a vocab matrix, I added one ready-made option for processing: an order-of-events game.

Link: bit.ly/RussiaRidge

Content

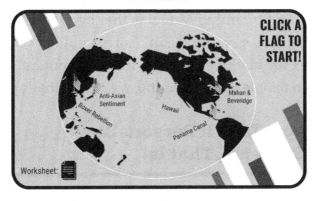

Each year, I've added a new option for how my US History class can study Manifest Destiny. Sometimes, it's just a link to a new video or primary source; I'm not trying to reinvent the wheel.

Link: bit.ly/manifestridge

Demonstrate

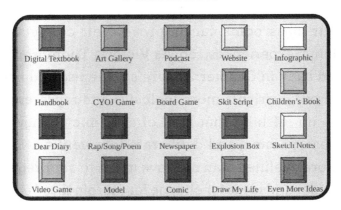

After my second year of teaching, I stopped giving students the option of writing papers to prove what they knew. I've added a variety of other ways they can demonstrate their learning.

Link: bit.ly/ridgeideas

Again, the whole point of slow-dripping differentiation in the Streaming Model is that by gradually giving students choice, we "brew up" (sorry, couldn't resist!) the chances for buy-in and sustained engagement. There's a reason people like streaming; we enjoy what's offered!

Strategy: Take It Personally (The Students, That Is)

Regardless of the genre, I think we can all agree that the best films and TV shows speak to our lived or imagined experiences. *Friends* resonated with those experiencing the paradox of being "alone together" in the Big Apple. *Black Mirror* spoke to living in the shadow of the internet and 21st-century technology. *Jurassic Park* brought out the kid in all of us and taught adults that some ideas are better left on paper.

Our classrooms can improve their connection to students' experiences, too. As Victoria Thompson mentioned back in Chapter 2, there's a deep-seated need to make our curricula more inclusive and representative. Make no mistake, that kind of systemic change takes purpose, passion, and deliberate intervention. Experts far more qualified than me have much to offer regarding strategies and ideas for change for marginalized communities in our schools.

What I can speak to, however, is the psychological connection our students can make to what they learn. In my classroom, it's a continual, day-to-day challenge. My favorite way to do this with students is using strategies like task cards. Each task asks students to build, reflect, or connect to what they've learned in a meaningful way. They can be embedded as in-lesson prompts or collaborative activities like Quiz, Quiz, Trade. They're designed with high schoolers in mind, but they could work with students of any grade level with just a few adjustments.

Meme It! Summarize what we've learned in a meme of your own design.	**I Still Wonder:** What questions do you still have about what we've learned?	**7 Word Summary:** Summarize what you already know about this topic in your own 7 words.
The Real World: Where do we see this reflected in today's world?	**Check-Up** Look at the faces below. Which matches how you're feeling before we start today's lesson? Explain why. ☺ ☺ ☺ ☹	**Sketch It!** Using drawings or other images, show what you've already know about this topic.
Haiku: Summarize what you've learned in a haiku. It's a poem of 5 syllables 7 syllables, And 5 syllables. (Note: it doesn't need to rhyme)	**What Changed?** How did your understanding change from when we started learning about this topic?	**Brain Dump:** Write everything you already know about a topic in 60 seconds.

Link here: bit.ly/ridgetasks

NATE'S NOTE: *These tasks should look familiar. They're meaningful processing activities adapted from Chapter 2! Notice how small tweaks to the Movie Theater Model can result in powerful moments that are much more student-centric.*

Strategy: Sudden Impact

If you're a subscriber to one of the many streaming services out there, one of the really neat side effects of getting hooked on a series is the connection you share with other viewers. It becomes a sort of new experience itself. When my students' favorite series airs, they crave talking about it with their friends the next day. Why? Students often enjoy the content just as much as they do its shared effect: friendship and community.

Students, just like adults, want learning to have an impact, some kind of connection beyond the experience of the moment. Just look at how superfans flock to ComicCon and Star Trek fans learn Klingon. Impact motivates us.

A caveat: not everything in our classrooms can or should be a big shared experience. But, we can think about sharing learning beyond our classroom walls. I like to think of what my students learn and do in my room like this:

Teacher-Centric	School-Centric	Community-Centric	Student-Centric
Teacher's use only.. Impact doesn't apply outside of the classroom.	Audience and impact extends to fellow students or teachers.	Applies to a local area or beyond. Affects people beyond the school.	Impacts students' lives directly and can be utilized in multiple settings.

Sometimes, students' work is just for us teachers. Not every exit ticket or warmup, for example, needs to extend beyond our four walls, but the more broadly applicable learning is, the more students tend to value it.

So how can we make learning apply outside of our Movie Theaters and Blockbusters? Here are a couple of quick examples:

Reciprocal Teaching: Have students make something to teach a peer how something works. Some of the best examples I use in teaching actually came from students. Case in point? Teaching mercantilism (an old form of economics) through a SpongeBob SquarePants metaphor.

See the example here: bit.ly/ridgesponge

Rent-an-Admin: Put your school administrators to work as an authentic audience for your students! Every admin (principal, vice-principal, dean of students, etc.) I've ever talked to has wanted to know what students are learning. An invite to the classroom is a win/win for both you and them. Although it can be intimidating to bring these folks into your classroom, you and your students can reap the rewards from greater visibility. (And let's be honest, your awesome teaching deserves to be seen!)

School Improvement DIY: Apply learning from your classroom to your local school and community, "do-it-yourself" style. One of my favorite lessons as a high school student was a project from my Advanced Placement Language teacher. At that time, a single standardized test score was used in Indiana to determine graduation eligibility. He challenged our class to figure out why standardized test scores disproportionately affected students of color in our building. We then created small groups to propose implementable solutions to address the issue, which started a months-long PBL (project-based learning) unit. He incorporated elements of literature like Johnathan Kozol's *Savage Inequalities*, statistics, and travel to other nearby school districts to examine as case studies. At the end of the project, my small group proposed a freshman mentorship program as a potential remedy. Our school admin at the time (2008) adopted our proposal, and now, as a teacher in the same high school I graduated from, the program is still thriving.

What I took from my own school improvement DIY experience as a student was witnessing how **classroom**

learning can directly affect my school community. Now, as a teacher in that same building, I get to ask a slightly different question: how can my classroom do the same?

Strategy: X-Ray

Amazon Prime Video has a really cool viewing feature called "X-Ray." If clicked, it pulls up quite a bit of information on what you're watching. On the screen, it overlays details such as character and actor names, connections and references to other films, and even goofs and errors made. It's a sort of peek behind the scenes that makes some of the more hidden parts of the film industry more visible.

X-Ray **IMDb**   Scenes   **In Scene**   Cast   Characters   Music   Trivia

Scene 1   Opening Credits   Starts at 00:00:00

What would it look like if we could "X-Ray" our instruction? What if we could take those invisible, implied parts of the classroom and reveal them directly to students and their families? Here are a couple of powerful things I've done in my own classroom that has had a big impact:

Brain Game: Teach students how their brains work and learn. When I poll my students every year with the question, "How many of you have been taught how studying works?" I'm consistently surprised by how few students respond yes. It's why I always take several days (a few at the beginning of the year and a couple more scattered throughout) to directly teach students everything from the basics of short-term memory to the effects of music on retrieval. If you'd like to see a sample of how I do this for students (at least the video version), check out this screencast here: bit.ly/ridgestudy

SEL (Social-Emotional Learning) Time: Give students time to work on social-emotional skills in your room. One of my biggest regrets as a beginning teacher was not spending more time as an undergrad studying the connection between students' social-emotional health and their learning. You might already have a self-created SEL program in your school or perhaps use an outside one like Calm Classroom (calmclassroom.com). I would also discourage thinking about SEL in your classroom as another thing to add to your plate. Instead, think of it like a marinade (to stick with a food metaphor). SEL works best when it's naturally "soaked-in" over time and just makes everything taste better!

One thing before we go on: of course, using the "X-Ray" strategy effectively depends upon personal comfort levels of sharing and students' readiness. For instance, some beginning teachers may not be ready on day one to suggest at-home study strategies for families. Some lower-age elementary students aren't going to benefit from a mini-lesson on ed psych. "X-Ray" works best when it's developmentally appropriate for all parties.

Plot ⤭ Twist

PLOT TWIST 3: Praxis Makes Perfect

If you hadn't picked up on it yet, we've talked a lot in this book about the need for *action and reflection*. They're the last—and perhaps the most crucial—component of the Streaming Model. Together, they form what the late educator Paulo Freire termed "praxis":

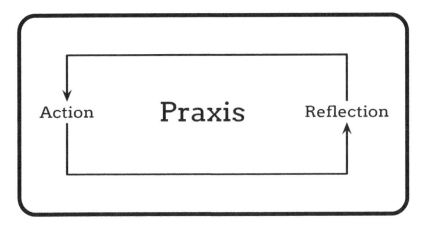

The takeaway on praxis is quick: so quick I can sum it up in one short paragraph. The truth is that not everything you're going to try in the Streaming Model may work— and that's okay. By testing and evaluating the tools and methods at our disposal, we have the opportunity to make students' learning experiences better. Praxis—the cycle of action and reflection—works because we can't "See What's Next" without looking back on where we've been.

Even if everything doesn't work perfectly every time (trust me, it won't), you can commit to acting, reflecting on your action, and acting based on your reflection.

Before finishing, let's be ~~kind and rewind~~ reflect and hit refresh: Let's summarize how we can Break the Blockbuster Model:

- **PLOT TWIST #1: Clone Your Classroom**

- **PLOT TWIST #2: Differentiate As Algorithms Do**

- **PLOT TWIST #3: Praxis Makes Perfect**

The question remaining: what comes next?

The Extended Universe

We began this book with Samuel B. Morse's telegraph question, *"WHAT HATH GOD WROUGHT?"* His question, when applied to the developments and challenges facing our classrooms today, seems yet to be determined. At first glance, it's hard to tell what the next ten, twenty-five, or fifty years will hold.

Morse, a man more concerned with communication than most, could never have envisioned the later inventions of pagers, dial-up internet, or Myspace, just like how we, at one time, couldn't have predicted these technologies or their eventual obsolescence. (Sorry, Tom!) At first glance, how our classrooms will appear seems much the same.

Trying to predict the future is only half the story. *Breaking the Blockbuster Model means not just thinking about what the future holds, but designing what we as teachers want that future to be.* We have the power to steer our reality towards a more equitable, accessible, relevant, and reflective place that benefits teachers, students, families, and administrators alike.

Think of it like *Back to the Future*. Marty McFly used a DeLorean, a car-turned-time-machine, to cruise all over the space-time continuum. We can do that, too. We can look back on the past while taking steps to get to the world we want to create. A few new inventions—the self-lacing sneakers of the education world—could take us there if we have the courage to stick our feet in.

Here's the honest truth. Just like the DeLorean did to travel through time, we need to hit 88 miles per hour and 1.21 gigawatts. Fast. The modern world is charging ahead and picking up momentum. In 2012, YouTube said one hour of content was being uploaded to their site every second. In 2022, that number jumped to more than eight hours.

Don't get me wrong. Changing and adapting our classrooms won't be without struggle and failure, as many of us who taught through COVID know. We were all forced to innovate and make leaps into the unknown. It took imaginative and persistent educators, administrators, and families to meet the needs of that crisis. The need to Break the Blockbuster Model will demand similarly innovative and bold risk-taking, like a hard look at long-standing pedagogical practices like direct instruction and detrimental impacts of long-standing traditions like textbooks, grades, and late-work penalties.

Perhaps the riskiest thing we could do, though, if we want to improve educational equity and accessibility, is take no risk at all.

BIBLIOGRAPHY

Agarwal, Pooja K., and Patrice M. Bain. *Powerful Teaching: Unleash the Science of Learning.* San Francisco, CA: Jossey-Bass, 2019.

Al Otaiba, S., C.M. Connor, J.S. Folsom, L. Greulich, J. Meadows, and Z. Li. "Assessment Data-Informed Guidance to Individualize Kindergarten Reading Instruction: Findings from a Cluster-Randomized Control Field Trial." *The Elementary School Journal* 111, no. 4 (2011): 535-560. doi: 10.1086/659031

Al-Azawei, Ahmed, Fabio Serenelli, and Karsten Lundqvist. "Universal Design for Learning (UDL): A Content Analysis of Peer Reviewed Journal Papers from 2012 to 2015." *Journal of the Scholarship of Teaching and Learning* 16, no. 3 (2016): 39–56. doi: 10.14434/josotl.v16i3.19295

Amabile, T. M. "The social psychology of creativity: A componential conceptualization." *Journal of Personality and Social Psychology* 45, no. 2 (1983): 357–376. doi: 10.1037/0022-3514.45.2.357

Atkinson, R.C., and R.M. Shiffrin. "Human Memory: A Proposed System and its Control Processes." In *Psychology of Learning and Motivation* 2 (1968): 89–195. doi: 10.1016/S0079-7421(08)60422-3

Bailey, J. P., and T.H. Williams-Black. "Differentiated instruction: Three teachers' perspectives." *Yearbook of the College Reading Association* 29 (2008): 133-151.

Behnke Y. "Textbook Effects and Efficacy." In *The Palgrave Handbook of Textbook Studies*, edited by Fuchs E., Bock A. (2018). doi:10.1057/978-1-137-53142-1_28

Bembenutty, Héfer. "Meaningful and Maladaptive Homework Practices: The role of Self-Efficacy and Self-Regulation." *Journal of Advanced Academics* 22, no. 3 (2011): 448–473.

Bennett, S., & Kalish, N. *The Case Against Homework: How Homework is Hurting Our Children and What We Can Do About It*. New York: Crown Publishers, 2006.

Bennett-Conroy, Waveline. "Engaging Parents of 8th Grade Students in Parent–Teacher Bidirectional Communication." *School Community Journal* 22, no. 2 (2012): 87–110. http://www.schoolcommunitynetwork.org/SCJ.aspx

Bierman, P., C. Massey, and C. Manduca. "Reconsidering the Textbook." *Eos Trans AGU* 87, no. 31 (2006): 306–306. doi:10.1029/2006EO310004

Bradley, Ben, Dan Restuccia, Chris Rudnicki, and Scott Bittle. "The Digital Edge: Middle-Skill Workers And Careers." *Burning Glass Technologies*, 2017.

Brighton, C. M., H.L. Hertberg, C. M. Callahan, C. A. Tomlinson, and T. R. Moon. "The Feasibility of High-end Learning in A Diverse Middle School." *Storrs: University of CT, The National Research Center on the Gifted and Talented* (2005).

Brookhart, Susan M. "Teachers' Grading: Practice and Theory." *Applied Measurement in Education* 7, no. 4 (1994): 279–301. doi: 10.1207/s15324818ame0704_2

Bruner, J. S. "The act of discovery." *Harvard Educational Review* 31 (1961): 21–32.

Cantrell, Steven, and Thomas J. Kane. "Ensuring Fair and Reliable Measures of Effective Teaching: Culminating Findings from the MET Project's Three-Year Study." *Bill & Melinda Gates Foundation*, 2013. https://usprogram.gatesfoundation.org/-/media/dataimport/resources/pdf/2016/12/met-ensuring-fair-and-reliable-measures-practitioner-brief.pdf

Capp, Matthew James. "The Effectiveness of Universal Design for Learning: A Meta-Analysis of Literature between 2013 and 2016." *International Journal of Inclusive Education*, 21, no. 8 (2017): 791-807. doi:10.1080/13603116.2017.1325074

Carifio, James, and T. Carey. "The Arguments and Data in Favor of Minimum Grading." *Mid-Western Educational Researcher* 25 (2013): 19-30.

Carr, N. S. "Increasing the Effectiveness of Homework for All Learners in the Inclusive Classroom." *School Community Journal*, 23, no. 1 (2013): 169–182.

Chetty, Raj, John N. Friedman, and Jonah E. Rockoff. "Measuring the Impacts of Teachers II: Teacher Value-Added and Student Outcomes in Adulthood." *American Economic Review* 104, no. 9 (2014): 2633–2679. doi: 10.3386/w19424

Cooper, H., and B. Nye. "Homework for Students with Learning Disabilities: The Implications of Research for Policy and Practice." *Journal of Learning Disabilities* 27 no. 8 (1994): 470–479. doi: 10.1177/002221949402700802

Cooper, H., J.C. Robinson, and E.A. Patall. "Does Homework Improve Academic Achievement? A Synthesis of Research, 1987–2003." *Review of Educational Research* 76 no. 1 (2006): 1–62.

Daniel, D.B., & Douglas, W. "E-Textbooks at What Cost? Performance and Use of Electronic v. Print Texts." *Computers & Education* 62, (2013): 18–23. doi: 10.1016/j.compedu.2012.10.016

Deslauriers Louis, Logan S McCarty, Kelly Miller, Kristina Callaghan, and Greg Kestin. "Measuring actual learning versus feeling of learning in response to being actively engaged in the classroom." *Proceedings of the National Academy of Sciences* 116, no. 39 (2019): 19251-19257. doi: 10.1073/pnas.1821936116

Docan-Morgan, Tony. "Positive and Negative Incentives in the Classroom: An Analysis of Grading Systems and Student Motivation." *Journal of Scholarship of Teaching and Learning* 6, no. 2 (2012): 21–40. https://scholarworks.iu.edu/journals/index.php/josotl/article/view/1668/1666

"Education in a Pandemic: The Disparate Impacts of COVID-19 on America's Students." U.S. Department of Education Office for Civil Rights, 2021. https://www2.ed.gov/about/offices/list/ocr/docs/20210608-impacts-of-covid19.pdf

Foley, Brian J., and Cameron B. Mcphee and M Consulting. "Students' Attitudes towards Science in Classes Using Hands-On or Textbook Based Curriculum." *AERA*, (2008): 1–12. http://www.csun.edu/~bfoley/Foley&McPhee%20AERA08.pdf

Goldberg, K. *The Homework Trap: How to Save the Sanity of Parents, Students, and Teachers*. Haddon Heights, NJ: Wyndmoor Press, 2012.

Good, Jessica, Julia Woodzicka, and Lylan Wingfield. "The Effects of Gender Stereotypic and Counter-Stereotypic Textbook Images on Science Performance." *The Journal of Social Psychology* 150, no. 2 (2010): 132-147. doi: 10.1080/00224540903366552

Hawkins, Vincent J. "Barriers to implementing differentiation: Lack of confidence, efficacy and perseverance." *New England Reading Association Journal* 44, no. 2 (2009): 11–16.

Hill, Phil. "How Much Do College Students Actually Pay For Textbooks?" *eLiterate*, 2015. https://eliterate.us/how-much-do-college-students-actually-pay-for-textbooks/

Huddlesson, Tom Jr. "Netflix didn't kill Blockbuster—how Netflix almost lost the movie rental wars." 2020. https://www.cnbc.com/2020/09/22/how-netflix-almost-lost-the-movie-rental-wars-to-blockbuster.html

Jensen, E. *Teaching with the Brain in Mind*. Alexandria, Va: Association for Supervision and Curriculum Development, 1998.

Khan, Al-Baab, Dr. Katherine Pieper, Dr. Stacy L. Smith, Marc Choueiti, Kevin Yao and Artur Tofan. "Missing & Maligned: The Reality of Muslims in Popular Global Movies." *USC Annenberg Inclusion Initiative* (2021). https://assets.uscannenberg.org/docs/aii-muslim-rep-global-film-2021-06-09.pdf

Kohn, A. "Abusing Research: The Study of Homework and other Examples." *Phi Delta Kappan* 88, no. 1 (2006): 9–22. doi: 10.1177/003172170608800105

Kohn, A. *Punished by Rewards: The Trouble with Gold Stars, Incentive Plans, A's, Praise, and Other Bribes*. Houghton, Mifflin and Company, 1993.

Kralovec, E., and J. Buell. *The End of Homework: How Homework Disrupts Families, Overburdens Children, and Limits Learning*. Boston, MA: Beacon Press, 2000.

Marsh, E. J., and H.E. Sink. "Access to handouts of presentation slides during lecture: Consequences for learning." *Applied Cognitive Psychology* 24, no.5 (2010): 691–706. doi: 10.1002/acp.1579

McNary, Sarah. *What Successful Teachers Do in Inclusive Classrooms: 60 Research-Based Teaching Strategies That Help Special Learners Succeed*. Thousand Oaks, CA: Corwin Press, 2005.

Miller, Matt, Angelia Ridgway, and Nate Ridgway. *Don't Ditch That Tech: Differentiated Instruction in a Digital World*. Dave Burgess Consulting, Inc, 2019.

Nightingale, Karl P., V. Anderson, S. Onens, Q. Fazil, H. Davies. "Developing the inclusive curriculum: Is supplementary lecture recording an effective approach in supporting students with Specific Learning Difficulties (SpLDs)?" *Computers & Education* 130 (2019): 13–25. doi: 10.1016/j.compedu.2018.11.006

Ok, Min Wook, Kavita Rao, Brian R. Bryant, and Dennis McDougall. "Universal Design for Learning in Pre-K to Grade 12 Classrooms: A Systematic Review of Research." *Exceptionality* 25, no. 2 (2017): 116-138. doi: 10.1080/09362835.2016.1196450

Patton, James R. "Practical Recommendations for Using Homework with Students with Learning Disabilities." *Journal of Learning Disabilities* 27, no. 9 (1994): 570–578. doi: 10.1177/002221949402700904

Redding, S. "Parents and learning." *International Academy of Education*, 2000.

Rockinson-Szapkiw, A. J. R., J. Courduff, K. Carter, D. Bennett. et al. "Electronic Versus Traditional Print Textbooks: A Comparison Study on the Influence of University Students' Learning." *Computers & Education* 63, (2013): 259–266. doi: 10.1016/j.compedu.2012.11.022

Rockoff, Jonah E., Brian A. Jacob, Thomas J. Kane, and Douglas O. Staiger. "Can You Recognize an Effective Teacher When You Recruit One?" *Education Finance and Policy* 6, no. 1 (2011): 43–74. doi: 10.3386/w14485

Santangelo, T., and C.A. Tomlinson. "The application of differentiated instruction in postsecondary environments: Benefits, challenges, and future directions." *International Journal of Teaching and Learning in Higher Education* 20, no. 3 (2009): 307–323.

Sharan, Y., and S. Sharan. "Expanding Cooperative Learning through Group Investigation" *New York: Teachers College Press*, 1992.

Shumow, L., E. Lyutykh, and J. A. Schmidt. "Predictors and Outcomes of Parental Involvement with High School Students in Science." *School Community Journal* 21, no. 2 (2011): 81–98. https://files.eric.ed.gov/fulltext/EJ957128.pdf

Smale-Jacobse, A. E., A. Meijer, M. Helms-Lorenz, and R. Maulana. "Differentiated Instruction in Secondary Education: A Systematic Review of Research Evidence." *Frontiers in Psychology* 10, no. 2366 (2019): 1–23. doi: 10.3389/fpsyg.2019.02366

"The Gauge Shows Streaming is Taking a Seat at the Table." The Nielsen Company, 2021. https://www.nielsen.com/us/en/insights/article/2021/the-gauge-shows-streaming-takes-a-seat-at-the-table/#methodology

"The UDL Guidelines." UDL, 2021. http://udlguidelines.cast.org/

Thomson, Andrew, Ruth Bridgstock, and Christiaan Willems. "'Teachers flipping out' beyond the online lecture: Maximising the educational potential of video." *Journal of Learning Design* 7, no. 3 (2014): 67–78.

Vatterott, Cathay. *Rethinking Homework: Best Practices That Support Diverse Needs*, 2nd Edition. ASCD, 2018.

Vygotsky, L. S. *Mind in Society: The Development of Higher Psychological Processes*. Massachusetts: Harvard University Press, 1978.

Weddle, Eric. "Interactive Map: Where Indiana Students Lack Home Internet, Computer." WFYI, 2020. https://www.wfyi.org/news/articles/map-where-indiana-students-lack-home-internet-computer

ACKNOWLEDGEMENTS

This book would not have been possible without the invaluable contributions of others. First and foremost, I'd like to thank the intellect, patience, and prodding of my wife, Annie, who was the source of countless ideas and inspiration. I'd also like to extend special thanks to my mother, Dr. Angelia Ridgway, foremost for her guidance as a parent but also for her suggestions that grace many of the following pages.

I also would like to thank Matt Miller, who's been an invaluable mentor and editor of this project from its beginning. I also owe Mairead Beeson and Najdan Mancic many thanks for their keen editing, illustrative skill, and ability to bring this book to life.

And last and most certainly not least, I would especially like to thank the educators who filled *Breaking the Blockbuster Model* with their voices, ideas, and strategies, including Patrice Bain, Benjamin Cogswell, David Frangiosa, Steve Heimler, Stacey Roshan, and Victoria Thompson. They are due much more credit and appreciation than what I can say here.

Bring Nate to Your School, District, or Event!

Bring *Breaking the Blockbuster Model* to your school, district, or event!

Professional Development doesn't have to be a drag. When you hire Nate to speak, you're giving your teachers engaging, practical, and personalized training they can use the next day. He's delivered keynotes, workshops, and conference sessions to thousands of teachers about pedagogy, edtech, and much more.

Schedule Nate to speak to your school, staff, or students. He offers everything from short hour-long sessions to day-long workshops.

Go to https://breakingblockbuster.com/work-with-nate/ and help him meet your needs!

Other Ways to Contact Nate:

✉ nate@teachingfromtheridge.com
🐦 @teachfromridge

ABOUT THE AUTHOR

Nate is a tech-loving history teacher, author, and speaker from Indianapolis, Indiana. He specializes in lesson design and differentiation and is licensed in History Ed and Mild Interventions. He was the Indiana Connected Educator of the Year in 2020, and his work has been featured in publications such as *The New York Times* and *The Washington Post*. He holds a Master's Degree in History from the University of Indianapolis.

Made in the USA
Monee, IL
09 July 2024

61570310R00103